"If ever there were a time to l'e, this is it. For those of us who r   st speak the truth to our non-Chri   ...instructs us to lace our words with kind....ss, gentleness, and self-control. Looking to communicate the truth of the gospel without being a pain in the neck? *Talk the Walk* will undoubtedly get you there."

Kendra Fletcher, Author of *Lost & Found: Losing Religion, Finding Grace* and *Leaving Legalism*

"Steve Brown knows that grace and truth are always flip sides of the same coin. In this touching and accessible book, he reminds us that prayerful tears are the most powerful way to share the gospel. As someone deeply interested in asserting Truth in a world full of false alternatives, I would eagerly put *Talk the Walk* in the hand of someone seeking answers."

Andrew Petiprin, Author of *Truth Matters: Knowing God and Yourself*

"I'm raising children and regularly wish to stick my head in the sand about the state of the world today, but . . . I'm raising children, so I can't. The Church is in desperate need of good, real conversations about what it looks like to stand on truth without wavering and exude grace without apologizing. *Talk the Walk* is just such a conversation starter, and I am grateful for it."

Jenni Young, Homeschooling mother; former Key Life staff member; blogger at KeyLife.org

"I have yet to figure out how to be confident enough to speak truth to people and yet humble enough to close my mouth when all I'm doing is showing off how smart I (foolishly) think I am. It's for this reason that I'm really thankful for this book. Steve is a wise and gentle pastor, and he'll help you (as he has me) feel the pinch of truth while he pours in the gentle love of the Christ who knows you. Get this book. Your unbelieving friends will thank you."

Elyse M. Fitzpatrick, Author and speaker

"Steve Brown's brilliant new book is a life-giving, irenic call to speak truth with the playful, kind ferocity of Jesus. Reading this book felt like taking a warm shower to rinse off the vitriol of ugly truthtellers and cleanse me of my own self-righteousness. This is a desperately needed book for a bitter and angry age."

Dan B. Allender, Professor of Counseling Psychology and Founding President, The Seattle School of Theology and Psychology; author of *The Wounded Heart* and *The Healing Path*

"Steve Brown does it again! A master at teaching grace, Steve gives us permission to believe and say what we Christians know and feel at the core of our being: 'We're right about Jesus!' Then Steve shows us how to hold to the truth in love and what that really means. This is Jesus's way of living. Don't miss this book—it is possible to be right without being insufferable!"

Pete Alwinson, Pastor Emeritus and executive director, FORGE

"I've always appreciated Steve's ability to hold close to his convictions while simultaneously avoiding the need to police others' behavior. In our highly divided times, we need voices like Steve's to guide us through the complexity of holding onto Christian truth while communicating it with love, humility, and humor. That's a rare gift."

Matt Johnson, Author of *Getting Jesus Wrong: Giving Up Spiritual Vitamins and Checklist Christianity*

"Ours is an increasingly post-Christian culture. For decades, old norms have been giving way to a new cultural ethos. For Christians, this new landscape has been disorienting and, at times, even discouraging. All too often, we've been tempted to respond with sharp and shrill expressions of fear rather than compassionate faith. In this timely and necessary book, Steve Brown shares how to be right the right way. I loved it."

Kevin Labby, Senior Pastor, Willow Creek Presbyterian Church

TALK THE WALK

HOW TO BE RIGHT WITHOUT
BEING INSUFFERABLE

Steve Brown

New
Growth
Press

WWW.NEWGROWTHPRESS.COM

New Growth Press, Greensboro, NC 27404
www.newgrowthpress.com
Copyright © 2019 by Steve Brown

Cover Design: Faceout Books, faceoutstudio.com
Interior Typesetting and eBook: LParnell Book Services, lparnell.com

ISBN: 978-1-948130-63-9 (print)
ISBN: 978-1-948130-64-6 (eBook)

Library of Congress Cataloging-in-Publication Data on file

Printed in the United States of America

26 25 24 23 22 21 20 19   1 2 3 4 5

To my beloved unbelieving friends
who are a lot closer to the kingdom than they think.

Contents

Introduction

The modern world says that it is impossible for a thinking person to have a metanarrative—an interpretation that accounts for all reality. There are smaller narratives within cultures and subcultures that are helpful and necessary for normal living. But a metanarrative—given the disagreements, the many ways of viewing reality, and the variety of heritages, backgrounds, races, and belief systems—is simply impossible. Further, it is arrogant and offensive to even suggest that there is one metanarrative.

At the risk of sounding arrogant and offensive, let me say here that there is, in fact, a true metanarrative. It is called the Christian faith. It is a stable, clear, and profound metanarrative.

Or to put it simply: Christians are right.

America and much of the world has gone through a massive cultural shift over the past thirty years. That shift is called postmodern, post-Christian, or perhaps transcultural. Whatever the name, the old and traditional views of anthropology, sexuality, social norms, religion, and culture have been set aside for the new views of tolerance, acceptance, and freedom.

Most thoughtful Christians I know are concerned about the cultural shift and feel, as it were, as if believers are standing

1

by a cliff, telling people to be careful. Those folks to whom Christians express their concern are tolerant, albeit dismissive. Believers stand by the cliff, giving their message, "Look at the blood down there. Don't get so close to the cliff! It will kill you." But folks keep jumping.

In the seventeenth century, Galileo was tried by the Inquisition and found guilty of heresy because of his teaching that the earth was not the center of the universe and, in fact, it moved around the sun. He was forced to recant his views (he needed the job and valued his life), but it is said that as he walked away from his trial, he muttered, "But it still moves." Christians are in that place now. Against an entire cultural shift that dismisses Christian verities as nonsense at best and outright lies at worst, Christians are still muttering, "Doesn't matter. It's still true. Truth isn't determined by a vote."

The cultural change is a tragedy of epic proportions if one believes (as I do) that the Christian faith is true—that it is not only true but the best thing to happen to human beings; that the Christian faith is about the unbelievably good news of God's love and forgiveness; that life is not meaningless or hopeless; that this is a way to live a reasonably full and joyful life; that people can live forever.

This is not a book about Christians being right and everybody else being wrong. It is about believing the right truth in the right way. The most dangerous thing about the Christian faith, for those who believe it, is the danger of being right. In fact, if believers do not learn to live and to speak right when we get it right, know when not to wave the red flag of our rightness in front of the unbelieving bull, and learn to manifest not only the truth of Jesus but his love and compassion, it will kill us and everything we love.

In this book I want to examine some of the less articulated truths of the Christian faith. For instance, while what I wrote about Christians being right is true, Christians should never forget the truth that all of us get it wrong—and some get it so wrong that the truth is no longer true. It is one thing to be right about the authority of Scripture, the incarnation of God in Christ, the resurrection, the Trinity, the substitutionary atonement of Christ, and eternal life, but at the same time, to miss the truths that have to do with humility, love, and forgiveness. Some of the meanest, most condemning and arrogant people on the face of the earth are Christians.

I know, because I am one of them. That makes me an expert.

This book is not written to correct you, but to remind me. I hope that along the way, God's Spirit convicts both of us. Someone has said that all preaching is, primarily, preaching to the preacher. Christian books are similar; they are just longer. What I have written here has taken me years to process.

If you want to hear truth spoken, by the way, it is probably best to listen to an old guy. I am as old as dirt. Old guys do not have anything left to protect; there is no advantage in spin for them. They do not want anything from you. I do not even care if you agree. Half of this book is probably wrong. I'm just not sure which half.

Kendra Fletcher in her book, *Lost and Found: Losing Religion, Finding Grace*, tells about a personal major life tragedy—a tragedy that gave her and her husband an "attack of sanity." She writes:

> How did we get to this point of a religious Christian life devoid of Jesus? How did the girl, raised in Fresno, California by first-generation believers fervent in their pursuit of Christ, and the boy, whose life was changed on a Santa Cruz mountainside during Young Life camp in high school, stray so far from the simple grace of the gospel and plunge headlong into religious self-righteousness?[1]

That is the question I want to pursue.

I have often spoken of a recurring dream. In my dream, God blows the whistle on the whole shooting match, history reaches its conclusion, and we are all standing before the Creator of all. We grow quiet as he speaks.

"I have some good news and some bad news for you."

"Tell us the bad news first," someone in the back (probably a Presbyterian) shouts.

"The bad news is that you were all wrong and some of you were incredibly wrong."

Then in my dream, God laughs (not the laughter of derision or irony but a free and joyous laughter) and says, "The good news is that I've talked to my Son about you. He says that he's taken care of it and you're okay. So . . . welcome home!"

CHAPTER 1

The Trail of Tears

And when he drew near and saw the city, he wept over it. (Luke 19:41)

In the mountains of North Carolina near Cherokee where I grew up, there is a wonderful outdoor theater. Every summer, they ran a production of *Unto These Hills*, a magnificent, dramatic presentation about the Cherokee Indians and the events that led up to the "Trail of Tears." The state and local militias forcibly removed the Cherokee Indians from their lands and homes to a designated Indian territory west of the Mississippi. On that march in 1838, the Indians suffered from disease, starvation, and horrible deprivation, and somewhere between two to six thousand of the 16,542 Cherokee perished. It is truly the "Trail of Tears."

The first time I had even heard of the "Trail of Tears" was as a teenager watching *Unto These Hills* for the first time. I was shocked, and then I wept. My wife and I have seen the play multiple times since; every single time, we have cried at the injustice, pain, and suffering of the Cherokee.

There are some things so horrible and difficult that tears are the only proper response. If there are no tears, there is either a misunderstanding of what one has encountered or a callousness that is troubling.

In Luke 19, Jesus had come to his beloved city of Jerusalem. As he looked out over the city, he wept. His tears were the reflection of God's tears for all humanity, and the cross is the ultimate manifestation of those tears. His tears were not that different from my tears while watching *Unto These Hills*, only multiplied a hundred thousand times.

Too often, Christians (myself included) have seen those who are not Christians as the enemy. One deals with an enemy by demonizing, demeaning, and dismissing. Conversations become debates, and relationships are chosen on the basis of who is on the Christians' side and who is not. Others may think Christians are angry, judgmental, and condemning, with the goal of taking way their freedom. Christians may be seen as old-fashioned, silly, and obscurantist.

Believe it or not, I understand the unbelievers. Frankly, we Christians do not have a wonderful track record. When we had the power, we used that leverage to manipulate, demean, and control others—just as unbelievers use power. However, when Christians use the leverage of power we violate the essence of the Christian faith.

One time, Jesus was discussing the inappropriate use of power and the leverage that comes from it. "You know," he said, "that the rulers of the Gentiles lord it over them, and their great ones exercise authority over them. It shall not be so among you" (Matthew 20:25–26). In other words, Jesus specifically commanded his followers who had power not to use it for leverage.

A friend of mine and I were discussing racism and its horrors. My friend said that he had become aware of his own racism when God woke him up in the middle of the night and convicted him. He laughed and said, "Do you know what God said? He told me that it was a lot worse than I thought. I didn't like anyone who wasn't like me." My friend said that after he thought about it, he repented. "The truth is that I don't like anyone whose skin isn't the same color as mine; who doesn't like the same music, books and movies I like; and who doesn't share my political views; and men who have hair when I don't. I don't even like someone who wears a shirt that doesn't match my fashion proclivities."

In Luke 9:50, one of Jesus's disciples says that he and the others had seen someone casting out demons in Jesus's name. This disciple tells Jesus that they had intervened, but Jesus's response is surprising. "Do not stop him," Jesus said, "for the one who is not against you is for you." Jesus was setting up an attitude for his disciples. He was showing how a Christian's reaction to the world should be radically different. For instance, in Matthew 5:43–45, Jesus said, "You have heard that it was said, 'You shall love your neighbor and hate your enemy.' But I say to you, Love your enemies and pray for those who persecute you, so that you may be sons of your Father who is in heaven." People who are not Christians are not enemies.

In Wendell Berry's novel, *Jayber Crow*, Jayber is the town barber in his beloved Port William. In order to make some extra money, Jayber works as a gravedigger and as a janitor at the local Methodist Church. One night he was tired and, as he often did, he takes a nap in one of the church pews he just cleaned. He has a dream. The church was filled with the people of Port William—the good and the bad, the adulterers and the families, the thieves and the businesspeople, the scoundrels and the church folks, and the ones Jayber liked and the ones he did not. When Jayber wakes up, he is surprised to find that he is weeping.[1]

This scene is a reminder of God's view of humankind, that he "makes his sun rise on the evil and on the good, and sends rain on the just and on the unjust" (Matthew 5:45b). God views all people with far more love than human, petty, and shallow self-interest. God knows where it hurts, and his compassion is far more universal. He knows about a world where hatred does not define humanity, where children are not used, where women are not abused, where people are not defined by how much they own and produce, and where the destruction, dark, and pain of sin does not touch everything. Jesus weeps over Jerusalem because he saw a world that could be but is not. There is enough evil, hatred, and pain in the world to solicit tears.

I experienced the kindness of tears from my high school history teacher. It happened when, after an exam, the teacher asked me to stay and talk with her. I figured that I was in trouble—again. Once the other students had left, the teacher came over to me and said, "Stephen, I'm disappointed in you." I wanted to say (but did not), "Get in line. Everybody else is disappointed in me too. You should meet my mother." Then the teacher said, holding the exam in her hand, "You could do a lot better than this." I was prepared to make some empty promises when I noticed something that astonished me. The teacher was crying and wiped the tears from her eyes. I did not know what to do with her tears. When the meeting was over, I was shaken.

From that day on, my grades in that class rose to amazing levels, even surprising me. In fact, I was afraid to show the grades to my mother because it would have given her a heart attack. I became a pretty good history student because of that teacher's tears. Tears are powerful communication tools.

Sometimes Christians forget the horrible pathos of the world. Paul says in Romans 8:19–23:

> For the creation waits with eager longing for the revealing of the sons of God. For the creation was subjected to futility, not willingly, but because of him who subjected it, in hope that the creation itself will be set free from its bondage to corruption and obtain the freedom

of the glory of the children of God. For we know that the whole creation has been groaning together in the pains of childbirth until now. And not only the creation, but we ourselves, who have the firstfruits of the Spirit, groan inwardly as we wait eagerly for adoption as sons, the redemption of our bodies.

Life is hard for everybody, including Christians. I have been a pastor for a lot of years and, because people are open with me about their secrets, I have been allowed to see the reality behind the masks that most people wear. I have buried a whole lot of babies, cleaned up after a whole lot of suicides, listened to a whole lot of confessions, and witnessed a whole lot of pain. The list goes on and on, and it has engulfed the universe. People live in a place of great pain. The world is dark for unbelievers and believers alike.

Christians really do have hope based in fact, faith based in a person, and freedom based in forgiveness and acceptance. "How often," Jesus said, in what might be the saddest statement he ever made, "would I have gathered your children together as a hen gathers her brood under her wings, *and you were not willing!*" (Matthew 23:37, emphasis added).

Christians love Jesus, the Bible says, because he first loved them—profoundly, deeply, and wholeheartedly. When believers hang out with Jesus, it is natural that they begin to respond to that kind of love *with* love. It is natural that believers start thinking the way Jesus thinks, caring about what he cares about, seeing things through his eyes, being angered when he is angered, laughing at things that are funny to him, and weeping where he weeps. In the face of a dark, lonely, painful, and fallen world, Christians grow to care and to shed tears.

Tears could make the difference in getting a hearing. It is important that truth be spoken, acts of mercy be shown, and sacrifice be definitive. I once opened a sermon to a large group of evangelical Christians by saying, "Millions of people are going to hell; and frankly, I don't give a rip." I was not bragging but confessing. I told them that I had friends who stood in malls and wept for the lost. "I don't even know their names," I said, "and so I don't care." After I had said that to this group of Christians, I repented and asked God to do something with my heart. This book is part of the result of God answering that request.

I was once the Bible teacher at a men's golfing retreat. The retreat was in a very poor country, but at one of the most luxurious resorts I have ever seen. The resort was surrounded on all sides by a fairly large fence that kept those in the resort from having to view the incredible poverty outside it. Sometimes I would go to the fence, raise myself up to the top, and look out over that poverty. It was a good way to ruin a vacation, and it ruined mine.

In fact, after a couple of days, I called a missionary friend in that country and begged him to come get me at the resort to let me spend a day with him. My wife and I spent almost an entire day walking the streets of that country and seeing starvation, malnutrition, disease, and great poverty housed in thrown-together shacks with no running water or sewerage. When I think back on it, I can still feel the sadness and helplessness I felt during that time.

At the golf retreat, I learned to understand something of the Bible, the heart of God, and the tears of Jesus. My fellow attendees and I were living in a resort and surrounded by pain. Once I saw these circumstances, condemnation was not the first order of business. Compassion and tears took priority. The trick was to learn to see through Jesus's eyes.

Believers and unbelievers weep beside open graves, deal with shattered dreams and abuse, face cancer, have shaming secrets, worry about their children, and live in fear. The reason Christians are different is the truth that defines them. Most of the time, that truth does not take away the pain, but to know that people are loved, accepted, forgiven, and eternal means that the "light shines in the darkness" (John 1:5). The Creator, despite the way it sometimes feels, says, "I know, child," shares pain, and is present to comfort. His presence makes all the difference.

Am I suggesting that we hedge the truth? Absolutely not! Jesus never backed off the truth. I also will say a lot in this book about Christians doing compassionate and good works in the world. If you had been with Jesus, you would have heard the sound of the blind men's beggar cups clanking on the rocks by the side of the road, and noticed the cripples' crutches thrown into the air as they danced. You would have rejoiced with the families of those whose loved ones were healed and, on at least two occasions, raised from the dead. Jesus calls his followers to the same work today.

Christians do compassion well. It is so important that they feed the hungry, clothe the naked, teach the unlearned, visit the prisons, and minister to the sick. The path of Christianity's growth in the world is marked by hospitals and schools. When God's people move in, slavery is condemned, women are affirmed, racial hatred ameliorated, and sex trafficking shamed. I know, I know, Christians have not always been the Christlike followers they ought to have been, but their record is far better than that of the critics who don't give a rip about the poor, the broken, and the abused.

When God's people were in exile in Babylon, Jeremiah the prophet told them to "seek the welfare of the city where I have sent you into exile, and pray to the LORD on its behalf" (Jeremiah 29:7). In a sense, Christians are in exile and "have no lasting city" (Hebrews 13:14) here. But it is incumbent on Christians to be a benediction in every place they live and work.

Being a blessing is not easy. It requires sacrifice. Jesus said in Matthew 16:24–26 that his followers should take up their cross (accept the sacrifice) and follow him. Speaking truth, doing good, and sacrificing are the places where Christians are called. It is their witness to the world.

At the beginning of this book, it is important that two things be clearly stated. First, sometimes Christians will hedge on the truth, not care enough to do the good works, and run from sacrifice. That is the reason for the cross. The blood of Christ covers all. That is called grace and it is the essence of truth. If Christians could be as good and as obedient as some would suggest they should be, God would have sent a book and certainly not his Son. You can tell how big a problem is by noting what it takes to fix it. Sin required the blood of God's own son.

Nobody I know lives up to what the Bible teaches. It is important to remember that the only people who get any better are those who know the truth that, if they never get any better, God will still love them. That is important. God's love will transform the message of condemnation and guilt into the real Christian message: people are great sinners, and Jesus is a great Savior.

Second, do not forget the tears. If Christians do not care, nobody will listen.

What follows talks about truth, compassion, and sacrifice in speaking to a world that does not want to hear. But if Christians forget the tears, that truth, compassion, and sacrifice will become nothing but arrogant, insufferable self-righteousness.

The difference is in the tears.

CHAPTER 2

The Gift of Truth

. . . speaking the truth in love, we are to grow up in every way into him who is the head, into Christ. (Ephesians 4:15)

A number of years ago, John Whitehead—an attorney, author, and The Rutherford Institute's founder and president—gave me a bumper sticker that read in big bold letters, "Speak Truth to Power." I put it on the back bumper of my car, right above my "Choose Life" Florida license plate. It confused my friends on the right who always suspected that I was a "closet liberal." And it confused my friends on the left who could not in their wildest dreams associate a pro-life message with that slogan.

There is the old joke about a businessman interviewing applicants for a position in his company. He asked each of them a simple question, "What is two plus two?" He got a variety of answers, including "I don't know, but I'm glad for the opportunity to discuss the issue," and a lawyer who referenced case law where two plus two was proven to be four. The final applicant got up from his chair, closed the door and the blinds, sat back down, leaned over the desk, and then whispered, "What do you want it to be?"

He got the job.

So often today, truth is whatever "you want it to be." Whatever you want it to be includes religion, gender, morals, marriage, race, and political truth. Not only that, but anybody who questions the freedom to make truth what one wants it to be is labeled intolerant, bigoted, or worse.

Have you ever had anyone say to you, when you have expressed a deeply held conviction or a truth that had changed your life, "I'm glad it's true for you"? What? I do not know anything that makes me spit and cuss more than someone speaking that kind of drivel. Frankly, I do not want to fly with a pilot, be treated by a doctor, or have a mechanic work on my car, who is that cavalier about aeronautical, medical, or mechanical truth.

So here at the beginning, let me make two statements that are quite controversial to a whole lot of people: there is true truth, and the Christian faith is true truth.

There Is True Truth

First, believe it or not, there is truth, and that truth is true apart from my perception or anyone's opinion. Winston Churchill is often quoted as saying that "The truth is incontrovertible. Malice may attack it, ignorance may deride it, but in the end, there it is." "True truth" (as my late friend and Christian apologist Francis Schaeffer called it) is not adjustable. I may not know that truth, I may miss it, and I may be wrong about it. But truth is there, and it is there aside from what anybody believes about it. For instance, God is personal, or he is not; you are forgiven, or you are not; I am loved by God, or I am not.

In a recent edition of *World Magazine*, Sophia Lee wrote about how some public intellectuals (Jordan Peterson, Ben

Shapiro, and Dennis Prager, who have a conservative and traditional message) are speaking and connecting with hundreds of thousands of young people who have lost their bearings:

> [N]either Peterson, Prager nor Shapiro are hawking new truths. Nothing they say is smack-in-head revelation. Instead, they seek to help people understand what they already know deep within their souls—timeless, elementary, common grace truths and values that are embedded into our very being, nature and substrata of consciousness. Their message won't save a single soul, but they appeal to people because of the law of God written on the listeners' hearts.[1]

Some things are simply true, and, in the silence of their hearts, most people suspect that they are true.

I know there are nuances to truth, and a lot depends on one's definition of truth. When Pilate asked Jesus, "What is truth?" (John 18:38), he was really asking two questions: *What is true?* and behind that, *What is truth?* For people who live real lives—those who are needy, lonely and scared spitless; those who have to make a living and pay the mortgage; those who have cancer; and those who struggle with building a bridge, fixing a refrigerator, or feeding a family—the fact of the existence of truth is not up for debate. The truth is that a cow is a cow, right is right, wrong is wrong, the sky is blue, and water is wet.

In 1964 Justice Potter Steward of the United States Supreme Court, in describing a test for obscenity in *Jacobellis v. Ohio*, said that he was not sure he could define pornography or obscenity but that he knew it when he saw it. That is how normal people deal with the fact that there is truth. Most people know that two plus two equals four, that love is better than hate, and that there is a difference between right and wrong.

I Am Right, and You Are Wrong

Not only is there truth that is true: what I have accepted, believed, and taught about the Christian faith is true; and if you do not accept it, you are wrong, and I am right.

Well, maybe not everything I have accepted, believed, and taught. I think my views on politics, movies, and restaurants are better than yours, but actually probably are not. There are points of theology, biblical exegesis, and certain doctrines where I could be wrong. In the basics of the Christian faith, however (those statements made in the Apostles' Creed), if you do not agree, you are wrong, and I am right.

There are times when I wish I was wrong. There are times when I do not want to speak the truth that I know to be true. There are times when the truth I know to be true causes me to wince. There are doctrinal truths that make everyone uncomfortable (e.g., the temperature of hell and the need for sacrifice). Nevertheless, the truth is the truth.

Does that sound arrogant? Maybe and maybe not. I have discovered that I have very little to be arrogant about. As someone has said, once you see truth you cannot simply unsee it. When Martin Luther (the lightning rod of the Protestant Reformation) was being brought to trial for his views and called to recant, he famously said, "Here I stand. I can do no other." That was not something he said because he wanted to say it or because he was arrogant when he said it. He was caught by the truth, and he could not change it. I am caught by the same truth.

I want to talk to those who are also caught by the truth, are convinced that it is true truth, and want others to see it. Mainly, we are going to talk about how to be right without being insufferable, and how to find a way to share the truths we know to be true with those whom we believe could benefit from the truths we know.

What follows will not be preaching to the pew, trying to convince someone who is already convinced. I suspect that if you are reading this book, you are probably already a Christian, affirm the truths of the Christian faith, and know that you have a responsibility to witness to those truths in the world. But we do need, on occasion, to be reminded. In fact, we need to be reminded more than we need to be taught—and certainly more than we need to be convinced. For this book's purposes, reviewing five truths will suffice.

1. There Really Is a God

There really is a God, he is in charge (the Creator, sustainer, and ruler of all), and people are not him. Paul's doxological statement at the end of Romans 11 should cause every Christian's stem cells to stand up and sing *The Hallelujah Chorus*: "'For who has known the mind of the Lord, or who has been his counselor? Or who has given a gift to him that he might be repaid?' For from him and through him and to him are all things. To him be glory forever. Amen" (Romans 11:34–36).

At the very heart of the Christian faith is the opening statement made by Rick Warren in *The Purpose Driven Life*: "It's not about you."[2] He says that people cannot fulfill what God has for them while, at the same time, trying to fulfill their own purposes. Rick Warren is right. Trying to fulfill your own purpose and God's purpose at the same time is like trying to pat your head and rub your stomach at the same time. Try it—you will see that I'm right.

2. God Has Not Remained Silent

The second truth makes the first truth more palatable: there is a God, and that God has not remained silent, uninvolved, or unconnected. The writer of Hebrews said, "Long ago, at many times and in many ways, God spoke to our fathers by the prophets, but in these last days he has spoken to us by his Son, whom he appointed the heir of all things, through whom also he created the world" (Hebrews 1:1–2).

The important issue for the Christian (and everybody else, even if they do not know it) is God's nature. Is he a monster?

Does he know me? Will he kill me if I do not do what he says? Does he know that I am hurt? Does he care? Does he love? And then, a hesitant question: Does he love *me*?

Bill and Gloria Gaither once gave a concert where a man sat with his wife in the front row, and obviously wanted to be anywhere else. His arms were folded, his eyes averted, and his entire demeanor was cold, angry, and hard. During that concert, the Gaithers sang a song they wrote (and one that has pretty much been sung in Christian circles everywhere), "I Am Loved." The thrust of the song was that now that I am loved, I can risk loving. The song ends with "We are loved!" and an invitation to walk together.

Just before singing that song, Bill asked audience members to take the hand of the person next to them while they sang the song together. The man kept his arms folded. He would not even hold his wife's hand.

During the intermission, the singers were all talking about that angry man on the front row. Bill decided that he was going to sing that song again at the end of the concert, but with a twist. He told people that while they were singing, they should hug the person next to them. Again, the angry man stood with a scowl on his face and his arms folded.

Then, to Bill's horror, Gloria left the stage and went out into the audience and approached the man. She threw caution to the wind and gave him a big hug.

The man broke down and wept.

The truth of God's love is unbelievable, amazing, and exciting. Love defines God (1 John 4:8). God loved the world so much that he gave his only Son. That is the basic truth of the Christian faith: God's love includes forgiveness, mercy, and compassion.

The problem with us Christians who have truth to share is that, when we talk about love, we either make it insipid and shallow, or we add a kicker to it (e.g., "God loves you, but don't let it go to your head!" "God loves you, but there is more to it than that" or maybe, "Now the ball is in your court, and that ball requires that you respond with goodness, obedience, and submission"). But watered-down love or conditional love are not the Christian faith, or the truth God gave us. God loved us with love that is hard as nails, driven into hands and feet, and without a kicker. It simply says, "I love you. Is that okay?"

3. God's Love Is Unreasonable

A sovereign God speaks his love. Nobody deserves it, but he loves people anyway. The Bible has a startling and negative view of human nature: "desperately sick" (Jeremiah 17:9); "None is righteous, no, not one" (Romans 3:10); our goodness is like "a polluted garment" (Isaiah 64:6); "all have sinned" (Romans 3:23). These are just some the descriptions the Bible uses to describe you and me. The counterintuitive and radical truth of the Christian faith is that God loves us despite our unlovable nature—and, surprisingly, because of our unlovable nature. Love in response to goodness is not love; it is reward. Love can only be experienced by someone who is unlovable.

All need to be loved and not one single person deserves it or ever has. Paul makes an obvious point in Romans 5 that sometimes there are those who will be willing to die for a good person, but that the astounding thing about Christ is that he died for the ungodly. That would be you and me.

Somehow, Christians have tried to fix those who do not want to hear the truth. Good heavens! We cannot even fix ourselves. I am an old preacher, and I have heard more confessions than any district attorney I know. Most of those confessions have come from people who have the reputation of righteousness. Believe it or not, because God has allowed me to move in the circles of well-known Christians, I have heard more confessions than you would believe by people you know—those who write books, stand in pulpits, pen Christian songs, and serve in significant positions of Christian leadership. What difference might it make if the people who did not want to hear the truth about sin knew that truth about you and me?

19

4. Christians Aren't Called to Be Fixers

Fixing people, making society more kind, forcing politicians and preachers to be good; correcting spurious views of right and wrong; changing the culture of death; and stopping racism, abuse, and hunger are way above a Christian's pay grade. Paul said to his young friend Timothy, "No soldier gets entangled in civilian pursuits, since his aim is to please the one who enlisted him" (2 Timothy 2:4). I am not suggesting (nor was Paul) that the public square should be free of Christians or Christian influence, or that Christians should not have dirty fingernails from their efforts of caring and service. Believers are called to bring their witness to the world, but the results of these efforts will be far more effective than reality will support.

The next chapter will address the importance of speaking and living truth, but for now it is important to remember that, as Jesus said, "[The Father] makes his sun to rise on the evil and on the good, and sends rain on the just and on the unjust" (Matthew 5:45). Further, God will deal with the good and the bad at the harvest, not now (Matthew 13:24–39). Christians cannot speak as outsiders of the human race. But utopian schemes—whether Christian, political, or pagan—are rarely effective, and much harm has been done by benevolent, visionary Christians and pagans alike. May God save us from those who think they know what is best for me, you, and everybody else.

5. Truths 1–4 Are the Main Thing

The final truth is quick and easy, and relates to the other truths: The first four truths are the main thing. Everything else is secondary. Other truths are important, but the primary should not be confused with the secondary. Believe it or not, sometimes the communication of truth begins with silence.

CHAPTER 3

The Sound of Silence

But he gave him no answer . . . so that the governor was
greatly amazed. (Matthew 27:14)

Christian truth is about as welcome in today's culture as a
wet shaggy dog shaking himself at the Miss America Pageant.
Truth does not matter, but intolerance does. If the subject is
salvation, Christian truth suggests that there are those who
are saved and those who are not. If the truth is about sin, then
some things are right and others are wrong. If it is about hell
and heaven, it means that one place is hot and the other is
not. If it is about forgiveness, then some are forgiven and others are not. Truth feels intolerant—and frankly, when I speak
Christian truth, it sometimes feels that way to me.

Truth, by its very nature, divides and offends. That is what
Jesus meant when he made the startling statement that he had
not come to bring peace but to set children against parents and
to create enemies of one's own household (Matthew 10:35–36).

The presupposition of this book is that Christians are
called to speak truth and, much of the time, to speak it to people who do not want to hear it. And they are constrained to do

so. Paul said in 1 Corinthians 9:16, "For if I preach the gospel, that gives me no ground for boasting. For necessity is laid upon me. Woe to me if I do not preach the gospel!" Paul was saying that he could not keep quiet.

Jeremiah the prophet had the same experience, "If I say, 'I will not mention him, or speak any more in his name,' there is in my heart as it were a burning fire shut up in my bones, and I am weary with holding it in, and I cannot" (Jeremiah 20:9). That is the normal experience of every Christian who knows the truth.

But with all of that being said, we Christians must be careful in what we say, how we say it, and even if we are to say it at all. Jesus cautioned that we should "not give dogs what is holy" nor "throw your pearls before pigs lest they trample them underfoot and turn to attack you" (Matthew 7:6). The truth we have is precious, dangerous, and explosively powerful in the way it can heal or hurt.

There are times when silence really is golden.

I have recently become a part of a small group Bible study at my church. I had never done that before, unless I led the Bible study. Because I am a seminary professor, write books, do media, and speak at conferences, those who do not know me are sometimes intimidated by what I do for a living. (If they only knew the truth.) Who I am makes it almost impossible to do normal things in the church.

My wife Anna and I, after praying about it, decided that we ought to be a part of one of the many small groups in our church. "Okay, we're supposed to do this," Anna said, "but honey, if we join a small group, you will have to keep your mouth shut." Anna is not afraid to say what she really thinks.

I have remained silent. In fact, Anna is quite proud of me and has told me so. I'm quite proud of myself, too. The truth is, I have the answers to a lot of the questions that come up in our small group. I know how to resolve many of the apparent inconsistencies of Scripture that are often mentioned, and when there are personal situations that come up—because I have been a pastor longer that most people in our group have been Christians and longer than a couple have been alive—I know what to do. I could teach our small group a thing or two because it is what I do for a living, and I am fairly good at it.

But I do not say a word—and only God, Anna, and I know how hard that has been. And just so you know, I love being a normal person, and I love the people in our small group. They have learned to love me too, without letting what I do interfere with who I am. I cannot tell you how much I value and love that small group of Christians.

Just as I have learned the value of silence in that small group and the benefits of that silence, all Christians need to learn is that sometimes there is great value in silence—even in their witness to the world.

Speaking Truth beyond Necessity

Silence, for instance, is better than saying too much that would be confusing and unduly irritating. A young seminary student was once asked to preach in a small country church. There was a major snowstorm, and only one farmer showed up for the service. The young preacher asked the farmer what he should do. The farmer told him that when only one of his cows showed at mealtime, he fed his cow.

The preacher—with only the one farmer in attendance—went through the entire service and preached an entire sermon. When the service was over, the student asked the farmer how he had done. "Son," said the farmer, "when one cow shows, I feed him . . . but I don't give him the whole load."

It is often enough to say, "Jesus loves you, and I do too." Other people do not always need to know the differences between Reformed and Arminian theology, the intricacies of the biblical view of law and grace, the Christian disagreements about biblical interpretation, or a Christian critique of politics and culture.

I recently was asked to visit an older man who, after a lifetime of atheism, was thinking about the Christian faith. He had started asking questions, and had even attempted to read the Bible each morning. We spent most of a morning talking about his questions. None of them had to do with theology, hermeneutics, culture, or disagreements within the Christian church—not one. Answering questions that are not asked, defining issues that are not raised, and going places that are not presently important is offensive and a waste of time. It is better that Christians remain silent.

Speaking Truth without Permission

Silence is also appropriate when a Christian has not been given permission to speak. Christians should not shilly-shally about who they are, and should at least give an indication of what they believe. But more information requires permission, and that permission is often given in the questions that are asked. If there are no questions and if no interest is expressed, it is wise to remain silent.

My friend Jake Luhrs, the front man for the Grammy-nominated metal band August Burns Red, is a Christian. Jake wrote a devotional book *Mountains*, and in it he writes:

> I never thought I'd write a book, let alone a devotional. To be honest, I didn't think the day would come when I would share some of my proudest (and not so proud) moments with an audience who might even care to listen. . . . If you know anything about me you know that I don't push "religion." I don't want to promote a religion, and I certainly don't want to hurt anyone with religion. But I do want people to have the same relationship I have with Jesus. I want them to feel loved and understood. When they're scared, I want them to see him as the ultimate source of love, hope, help, strength and forgiveness.[1]

Why did Jake write his book? He did it because so many of his fans had questions. In fact, he formed a nonprofit community called HeartSupport that touches 70,000 people each month with counseling, help, and acceptance. He started that community and wrote the devotional book because so many people granted permission. Jake told me that when he was on tour, there were so many who wanted to know about his faith, but because of the tour and the necessity of moving quickly to the next city, he simply did not have the time to say what needed to be said and to answer the questions that had been asked.

Christians do not have to give others the whole load. When asked, Christians can say, "Yeah, I am a believer, and it's the most important thing in my life. If you ever want to hear about it, just ask and I'll tell you." Or in my case as a religious professional, when I am asked what I do, I sometimes answer, "I tell people *who want to hear* about Jesus." Or perhaps when Christians think they have a message that will help someone in trouble, they can say, "If you want me to, I'll be glad to share it with you." Permission opens the door to speaking truth. If permission is not given, silence is a good practice. Silence is also a wise practice when spoken truth is spoken for the wrong reasons.

Speaking Truth from Guilt

There are Christians who feel guilty about not speaking the truth. Perhaps they have heard some preacher or Christian leader say that their friends know about their work, their golf score, and the beer they drink, but they do not know the most important thing about their lives—their relationship with Christ. So then, out of guilt, they decide to tell everybody they know. And because they are doing it out of guilt, they generally do it horribly wrong.

I have been there and done that. I got a seminary degree from a liberal graduate school. It's a long story, but eventually the Spirit changed my beliefs. I became quite orthodox in my views on the Bible and the Christian faith. I felt guilty that I had not told anybody, and I made a promise to God (a really dumb thing to do and a sure way to significantly increase my guilt quotient) that I would be his witness to those "confused liberals." I did, and do you know what happened? I was dismissed. One of my friends said that I was going through exams (I was at the time) and just looking for a warm fuzzy place, and found it in the silly, obscurantist beliefs of my childhood.

If you are reading this book because you feel guilty about not speaking truth, let me suggest that you continue not speaking truth. Guilt makes communication phony and shallow, and often causes people to use a cannon when a BB gun would do. The worst Pharisees I know are those whose arrogance and condemnation of others comes from their own guilt in not being a faithful witness—as well as, I might say, a pile of other shame and guilt issues.

Let me give you a principle: Guilty people make others feel guilty. Free people make people feel free. Because of those truths, if people have not experienced the freedom of unconditional forgiveness that is at the heart of the Christian faith, remaining silent is best.

Speaking Truth to Get Power

Some Christians are looking for power over others by being right, and speaking truth is the way to get it. I have been involved in debates for most of my life. A lot of that was in academic circles; and I was once president of a college debate club. I did it for fun, often taking positions that were not mine, just so I could argue about them. And more often than not, I won the debates or prevailed in the argument, not because I am that smart but because I have a glib tongue and a deep voice.

After I became a Christian, I brought those "gifts" into the Christian arena. I remember one time when participating in Evangelism Explosion training (an evangelistic ministry founded by the late James Kennedy). I went with two others (another man my age and an elderly woman who was our trainer) to visit a man and his roommates who had gone to the church, given their address, and indicated they were open to a contact. We introduced ourselves and promptly, as we were trained to do, turned the conversation to God. The young man said, "I used to believe that stuff but don't anymore." I asked him specifically what he did not believe and when he told me, I showed him the shallowness of his views and the profound nature of mine. When I turned to talk to his roommate, he said, rather loudly, "Whew!"

When my friends and I left the apartment, I suggested that the man would not dare debate a Christian again. "You're probably right," responded the trainer, "because they won't have anything to do with Christians again." Of course, she was right. I was young, and it felt good to strike a blow for God. After all, I was a warrior for God, and I had won the battle.

As I already said, Christians are right, and others are wrong. That is actually true and very dangerous. Frankly, even writing those words made me feel self-righteous, and I am glad to be on the winning side. Another chapter addresses this in more depth, but so you know, I repented of my self-righteousness. I also decided that, in this case, silence is golden.

Speaking Truth from Self-Interest

Silence is also golden when we speak with an agenda of self-interest. A number of years ago, I had a friend who had become an evangelist. As his friend, I knew that he did not buy anything he was preaching and asked him about it. "Of course, I don't believe it," he said, "but I don't know a better way to meet girls and make great money." He may have been speaking truth to those who came to hear him speak (even if he did not believe that truth), but the reasons for speaking that truth meant that eventually those who listened would turn away and run.

Paul wrote from a prison cell, "Some indeed preach Christ from envy and rivalry, but others from good will. The latter do it out of love, knowing that I am put here for the defense of the gospel. The former proclaim Christ out of rivalry, not sincerely but thinking to afflict me in my imprisonment. What then? Only that in very way, whether in pretense or in truth, Christ is proclaimed, and in that I rejoice" (Philippians 1:15–18). Paul was teaching how God is sovereign and sometimes uses all kinds of motivations to glorify his name; he was not presenting a case for rivalry, selfish ambition, lack of sincerity, and pretense.

When Christians speak truth, it would be a wise practice to ask themselves, *What is in this for me?* If they find an answer to that, it is best to keep quiet. If they discover that their agenda is to gain acceptance from their Christian friends, to be a part of the in-crowd, to ameliorate guilt, to prepare the ground for a sales pitch, to get the religious vote, to get a date, or to impress others with their spirituality, Christians might remember that sometimes silence really is golden.

Speaking Truth from Ignorance

There are others who try to bring their witness of truth to the people they know, yet are simply not very informed about the nature of the truth they speak. When that happens, it is better to remain silent than to keep talking.

As a pastor, I conducted "skeptics forums," where I met with atheists and agnostics on a regular basis to discuss and debate issues of faith. The whole effort started because there were so many new Christians in my church who knew they had been forgiven, loved, and changed, but who knew very little more than that. Their husbands, wives, boyfriends, girlfriends, and acquaintances often reacted to their change by confronting these new Christians with questions for which they had no answer.

I designed the skeptics forum as a place where those new Christians could refer their hostile friends and family members.

If these loved ones really wanted answers, they could find them there. The new Christians were advised to not try and answer the questions for which they had no answers. Instead, they were to say, "Look, I'm new at this and I don't have answers to your questions, but my pastor does and he's meeting with people like you every Monday evening."

Christians, of course, should be growing in their understanding and knowledge of the Christian faith. That goes without saying. Not only that, but until those Christians acquire cogent, rational, biblical, and clear answers to questions that are asked, it is really okay to say, "I don't have the foggiest idea," "I'll check and get some answers for you on that," or "I wish I knew enough to speak to that issue but I'll ask someone who knows; but for now, let me tell you how wonderful it is to know I'm forgiven." In that case, silence is golden.

In John 9, Jesus healed a man who was born blind, and it caused all kinds of controversy. Those who hated Jesus questioned the parents, brought up theological issues about God's glory, checked to see if the blind man was lying, tried to punch holes in his testimony, and talked about human sin and God's refusal to act in the presence of a sinner like Jesus. The man who had been healed said simply, "Whether he is a sinner I do not know. One thing I do know, that though I was blind, now I see" (John 9:25).

Because the religious leaders had trouble countering a clear and demonstrable truth, they kicked the man out, and he promptly ran to Jesus. Jesus did not tell him what he could have said to the leaders. Jesus did not give the formerly blind man a lesson in Apologetics 101, nor correct his theological misunderstanding. Jesus just accepted him.

Say what you know and have experienced. It is enough.

Speaking Truth to Help God Out

Here is comforting and disturbing truth: God does not need anyone. In fact, he was doing fine before people came along, and he will do fine after they gone. People are just not that important. If it were not for his love and the value he places on his own (Psalm 116:15), people probably would not even leave a hole where they die, as the old anecdote says:

> "Where's Jimmy?" asked the customer to the manager of the general store.
> "Jimmy is no longer with us," the manager replied.
> "Who took his place?"
> "Jimmy didn't leave no place."

God is going to do what he is going to do—and if he wanted to, he could do it by himself. But because he loves us he lets have a part in sharing his love and grace with the world. Ultimately, nobody will misunderstand the truth because Christians did not say it right, and nobody will be lost for eternity because Christians were unfaithful. God is bigger than our mistakes and misstatements. It's the Spirit who draws people to God. How else to explain why anyone would admit that they are a sinner with no hope of saving themselves? Humans don't do that without divine intervention.

That kind of bothers me because I would like to get a little bit of the credit. On the other hand, it is a great deal of relief to know that I do not have to be God anymore. Actually, when I make myself too important and think that I am "helping God," he leaves the room and lets me do it myself. And more often than not, disastrous results ensue.

Speaking Truth with Silence

Sometimes it is best to be silent and to let love, freedom, and joy do the talking. There are some things Christians cannot say without words, but there are other matters that are only confused by words. My wife, who is a musician, has often said to me that music is the universal language. Sometimes it is best to remain silent and hear the language of music. Just so, sometimes it is best to speak the language of silence.

It is a cliché, but nevertheless there is some truth to believing that Christians are the only Bible unbelievers ever read. However, with due respect to that point of view, let me say that most of us sin so much, betray our principles so often, and fail so obviously in our Christian walk that the message is mixed and muddled.

But what if we remained silent by not defending ourselves? What if we remained silent when others are condemning those whose lifestyle, politics, or religious views are deemed unacceptable? What if we remained silent and refused to be the social, political, and religious critic of every opinion that wasn't our own? What if we remained silent in the face of rejection? What if we refused to share the secrets we've been told or tell the stories we've overheard? What if we remained silent and overlooked the foibles of others? What if we looked at the pain of our neighbor and just loved him or her, instead trying to fix the unfixable? What if our response to confusion, fear, and guilt was simply, "I know"?

There is a powerful witness in that kind of silence.

CHAPTER 4

Watered-Down Wine

For we did not follow cleverly devised myths when we
made known to you the power and coming of our Lord
Jesus Christ, but we were eyewitnesses of his majesty.
(2 Peter 1:16)

My friend Kent Keller, pastor of Kendall Presbyterian Church
in Miami, once commented on 2 Peter 1:16 above: "This isn't
Hollywood. Christianity is an historical faith, grounded in
acts and facts: real people, real events, real time, real places.
That's the story the Bible gives us. Take it or leave it. Love it or
hate it. Accept it or reject it. But you don't get to mess around
with it, edit it or rearrange it so that it's more to your liking. It's
not a majority thing. Truth stands on its own."

Of course, Kent is right—and therein is an enormous problem and an ever-present danger. I don't want to belabor the
point about truth, but more does need to be said. Kent was
simply saying that we shouldn't take the wine—rich, delightful
and expensive—and mix it with water. It's not the real deal.

I heard Gloria Gaither once say that it was dangerous to want to be with the cool kids, but it is a human instinct to want to be liked and to have one's views affirmed (i.e., to be cool). Therein is one of the major dangers of speaking truth. If Christians change the truth, that truth will not make any difference. If Christians are not very careful in their efforts to make the truth palatable (which is a good thing to do), they can move to beliefs that are not the Christian faith—only a reasonable facsimile. If Christians are not careful, they can make the short step from changing the packaging to changing the product.

With music, the note "A" is the same whether it is sung or played in the music of "Bach, Bubba, and the Blues Brothers."[1] The same is true for Christian doctrine. The song/message/truth of Christ comes in a lot of different formats, but the truth should never change. However, the problem with the format is that one must always be careful that it enhances the message and does not change it. It is important that Christians be sensitive to culture, to offensive ways of communicating to that culture, and to the presuppositions of that culture, but the truth itself simply cannot be compromised.

Let me now say some things about the nature of the truth.

Real Truth Is Practical

Spoken and lived truth, by nature, is practical. Truth is not true because it works; truth works because it is true. I teach preaching to seminary students, and one of the important things I teach them is the "so what?" principle. Preachers should start with the Bible, read the commentaries, and exegete the text properly. I then suggest that as they prepare the sermon, they should remember that great preaching always has an answer to the question, "So what?" If there is no answer to that question, Christians should keep truth to themselves.

We Christians are long on doctrinal truth and short on the practical implications of that truth. One of the really important ways Christians communicate our truth is not so much by being pure, righteous, and good. Those things have value, but our truth is better communicated practically. Christians can show how we sleep at night, the balance we have in our lives, and the joy of being loved. We can also be authentic when we do not sleep well, are not very balanced, and do not feel a lot of joy. There is something very attractive and practical about being forgiven and free.

One of the really spurious things Christians believe is that a Christian has to go through hell to get to heaven, and that an unbeliever gets to go through heaven to get to hell. I have a pastor friend who says that the problem with the church is that we all have our noses up against the windows of the church looking out and fantasizing about how much we would like to be "out there." He says that we will really understand the gospel when the unbelievers have their noses up against the widows of the church fantasizing about how much they would like to be "in there."

Real Truth Is Therapeutic

Spoken and lived truth is also therapeutic. Truth often cuts before it heals.

Many years ago, as a young pastor in a village on Cape Cod, a Roman Catholic priest friend and I decided to have a covered-dish supper. The ecumenical movement was in at the time and I was not only the pastor of the Protestant church in the village at the time; I was also a student at a seminary in Boston, where everyone bemoaned the divisions in the church. My friend and I had our covered-dish supper with two other Catholic priests and two Protestant ministers, joining together at a panel after dinner. It was a grand affair, all sweetness and light. We talked about how much we loved each other, how much we had in common, and how horrible our divisions were.

Then, my late mentor Dr. John Stanton (a member of the small church I served) threw a bomb in our playground.

He stood up and said, "Could I say something?" I was the moderator and was not about to deny him that opportunity. "I've really enjoyed this discussion," he said, "but frankly I'm bored. There are some things that need to be mentioned and nobody has brought them up. I have a list." He then proceeded to talk about the serious differences between Catholics and Protestants, and then said, "Until we talk about these issues, this meeting is nice but of no import whatsoever."

I thought that the meeting would end quickly. Just the opposite happened. John spoke truth, and the whole idea of brothers and sisters in Christ in our little village took on real meaning. Loving each other became the norm—not despite our differences, but because of them and Jesus.

I once spent a long time talking with the editor of a magazine created primarily for the gay and lesbian community. He did not say so, but I knew he planned to do a hit piece about a friend of mine who had been quite vocal on sexual issues and held a position quite different from the editor. The first thing I told the editor was that what I was going to say was in no way a judgment on him, his views, or his lifestyle. "When someone is as screwed up as I am, one doesn't throw rocks at anybody," I said, "and I'm more screwed up and sinful than anybody I know."

Then, I began to give him a lesson in Christian beliefs about truth in general and sexuality in particular, trying to explain about revealed truth and how Christians—if they are the real deal—are not free to change those view on a whim, even if we are incapable of living up to those truths. I said a lot more than that (and I will say it later in this book), but when we finished talking he said, "I didn't understand, and I kind of get where you're coming from." The magazine did not publish the hit piece.

Compromised Truth Fizzles

Spoken and lived truth is devastating and destructive when it is compromised. Sarah Condon is one of the funniest and most insightful Christian communicators around. In her book, *Churchy*, she tells of a difficult time in her life:

> Some years ago I walked into a church in desperate need of a good word. A dear friend had died violently, and I was hoping the preacher would give me something, anything, to console me. In the Scripture for that morning, Jesus had appeared before his friends after being crucified. He came to offer them comfort and the promise of the Holy Spirit. "This is exactly what I need," I remember thinking to myself. Then the preacher stood in the pulpit and offered next to nothing. He related a story about an old car he had and how much that car had been through (you know, like wrecks) and how much he loved his car and how his car had scars just like Jesus. "We all have scars," he insisted, "just like the scars of Jesus. Hopefully that's a comfort to you." I just sat there and thought "If that's all you got, then I'm screwed." I need Jesus to be Jesus.[2]

One time, Jesus was teaching about God's goodness and said something that has haunted and encouraged me ever since I first read it: "[W]hich one of you, if his son asks him for bread, will give him a stone? Or if he asks for a fish, will give him a serpent? If you then, who are evil, know how to give good gifts to your children, how much more will your Father who is in heaven give good things to those who ask him!" (Matthew 7:9–11). My father, who was not a good person by human standards, loved me as much or more than anybody I have ever known. He did not think it was possible to have a party unless I was there. When I first read those words of Jesus

I thought, "If God loves me one-fifth as much as my father loved me, I'm good to go and everything is a lot better than I ever thought."

Later, as I entered formal ministry, those words—still personally of great comfort—took on another meaning. Even evil people (i.e., everyone) give good things (i.e., the truth) to their children, and that is a good thing. The tragedy, using the imagery of Jesus, is that people so often give instead a stone or a serpent (i.e., lies). The stones are sometimes pretty stones and the serpents sometimes look like Puff the Magic Dragon, but they are useless and even dangerous. Only the truth heals, frees, and redeems. Anything else might make people feel good, but it is useless and destructive.

Real Truth Divides

Spoken and lived truth is also a main indicator of when Christians should no longer speak that truth to those who do not want to hear it. When the real truth (not watered-down truth) is spoken, the reaction to that truth is an indication of whether Christians follow up with more truth or, on the other hand, are granted permission by Jesus to walk away.

Jesus had some clear instruction for believers when they encounter those who just want to be left alone: they should just walk away, and shake the dust off their feet (Matthew 10:14). If time is limited (and it is), and there are some who want to hear and some who do not want to hear (and there are), then Christians need to walk away from those who do not want to hear and go to those who do.

Real truth sometimes divides and sends people away. When I was a young pastor and beginning to change my theological views, the church where I served had a brand-new missions committee.

At the first committee meeting, there was a lady with a shocked look on her face. "Let me see if I get this right," she said, "we're saying that other religions are wrong and ours is

right and we're going to try and convert them to our religion."
I started to say "duh," but did not. She went on, "If that's what
we're saying, I can't participate, and I'm out of here." With
that, she got her coat and purse, and walked out the door.

Was that bad? No, that was good, and if I knew what I
know now, I would have gotten a bottle of champagne and
celebrated. I now know that some people bring renewal to the
church by joining it, and others bring renewal to the church
by leaving. Just so, sometimes Christians are not supposed to
speak truth to some people who do not want to hear.

Walking away is really hard for a certain kind of person.
Those "type A" kinds of Christians just never give up and, I
might say, never shut up. I once had a man say to me that he
felt that the only reason I was his friend was to "win him to
Christ." He said, "I like you and I want to be your friend, but
can we still be friends and disagree about something as important to you as Christ?" We did remain friends, but I never again
brought up my faith. I had already said all I needed to say, and
I told him that if he ever wanted to talk about it, we could;
until then, we would just be friends. He eventually did become
a Christian, but I was not the one who got him there (now, that
is irritating).

I have a friend, Roe Brooks, who was a staff member at the
old Campus Crusade for Christ (now Cru—he started back in
1952). He was assigned Harvard University as his mission field.
Roe is one of those people who is big, has a winsome smile as
big as himself, and does not have a shy bone in his body. They
said that when Roe came on the campus of Harvard, students
would quickly scatter.

One even hid behind a tree. Roe saw him and went over to
him. "Roe," the student said, "I like you, but leave me alone. I
don't want to hear any more about Jesus."

"I understand that," Roe said. "Let me pray for you." The
student bowed his head, and Roe prayed, "Lord, I have a man
here who doesn't ever want to hear about you ever again, and

I ask in the name of Jesus that you give him what he wants. From now on, please leave him alone and never. . . ."

The student pulled on Roe's coat, interrupting the prayer, and said, "Wait Roe, I wouldn't go that far."

But if someone really does want to go "that far," let them. Christians need to first check and see if unbelievers want to go further; but once it is clear that they have drawn a line, for God's sake, do not cross it. Do not say, "Okay, if you want to roast in hell, it's your responsibility." That gives the impression that Christians know who is going to hell, and that they are kind of glad others are getting what they deserve. The truth is, *Christians* are not going to get what they deserve—because God has this unreasonable love for them that nobody can explain. When believers know that there are those who refuse God's love, there is no joy in that reality.

CHAPTER 5

When Truth Gets Personal

I am the way, and the truth, and the life. (John 14:6)

Some people think I am prideful and arrogant—and they are right. They do not even know the half of it. I sometimes struggle with humility, which is kind of surprising given that I hardly know anybody who has more reason to be humble than I do. However, there is one area where I sound arrogant and prideful, and actually I am not: Jesus likes me a lot, and I honestly think that he likes me more than he likes you—about ten percent more.

Lest you criticize what I just said too harshly, the fact is that if you cannot say the same thing I just said, you probably have not understood the essence of the Christian faith. Believers are like a bunch of children saying to one another, "Dad loves me more than he loves you! I'm his favorite." Christians have the sort of father who makes them all feel that way.

I just talked to a friend of mine who asked me what I was doing, and I told him what I had just written in the above paragraph. He laughed, and then told me about his mother's funeral. His mother Corabel was a wonderful lady, and at the funeral, a woman came up to him and said that she had been Corabel's closest friend. "We loved each other and have been prayer partners for years. She was a truly wonderful woman. I'm going to miss her so much." My friend thought that was a nice thing to say. And then another person came up to him and said exactly the same thing, then another, and another—until a dozen people had affirmed their "best friend" status and that they were prayer partners.

Corabel's love for people was incredible, and she always made others feel special because of it. That is how Jesus loves his own.

Most effective Sunday school curriculum writers have made sure that children see Jesus—his kindness, gentleness, and love—as more important than his moral and ethical teachings, his comments about theological truth, or his cleaning out the money changers in the temple. That is wise in teaching children; but it is just as wise in anyone's journey. Properly understood, getting to know the story of Jesus (a nonfiction story) and his love is the starting and ending point for Christians. It should be the starting point for the communication of Christian truth.

In fact, God leads with the message of Jesus's love. Christians really do love him because he first loved us (1 John 4:19). It is the story of his love and how Christians experience that love—absolute, unconditional, and eternal—that makes all the difference in how Christians interact with unbelievers. Christians are not communicating—they are introducing. I do not have a theology to share but a friend to meet. Theology is important, but that is not a good place to begin.

In the following chapters, I will say a lot about heart attitude because communicating and living the truth to people who do not want to hear or see it is 95 percent attitude and 5 percent technique, knowledge, planning, and training. Actually, attitude may be enough. Paul said that Christians have the "mind of Christ" (1 Corinthians 2:16), and said in Philippians 2:5 that they should "have this mind among yourselves, which is yours in Christ Jesus." Sharing truth is not so much about what Christians do, how much they know, or how smart and good they are; it is an attitude. The attitude starts with Jesus. Christians are called to smell like Jesus. When that happens, maybe what Jesus said about people being drawn to him would become far more apparent.

Key Life, the ministry with which I am associated, for two or three years helped sponsor a national event called Grace Encounter. It started when a pastor friend of mine Jerry Parries and I were having lunch. We love each other, and both of us feel better when we hang out together. At that time, there were riots in a good deal of the country, and the group Black Lives Matter was getting a whole lot of press. Jerry is black, and I am white.

It was natural that our conversation turned to the prominent racial divisions that were headlined at the time. That led to questions about what Christians should do, and why a black guy and white guy loved each other so much. We decided that it was because of Jesus. Jerry and I are both quite needy and sinful, and we have political ideas that are not always in agreement. But we both know that Jesus loves us when neither of us deserves it. That enables and motivates our love for each other.

Jerry's church and another local church sponsored a conference and have developed a wonderful relationship. The two pastors—Jerry, the pastor of The Christian Family Worship Center, and my friend and pastor Kevin Labby, of Willow Creek Church (Winter Springs, FL)—have become close friends, and so have the people in the two churches. We have had worship services together; the worship teams and bands from each church have also led worship in each other's church. The pastors have exchanged pulpits. We have shared a church picnic; and The Christian Family Worship Center has been holding their worship services in the Willow Creek Church building, after selling their old building and needing a place to worship before buying or building a new facility.

Now here is the principle behind Grace Encounter: racial reconciliation—and anything else of eternal importance—is an illustration, not a focus. Throughout all of the conference planning, both churches strongly agreed that they were not holding a racial conference, but one on the radical grace and love of Jesus for screwed-up people who did not deserve it.

People are always saying to me that, while they are glad for the message of God's radical grace, Christians must be careful because people will take advantage of it. These people say that grace sometimes appears to be a license to sin. They say that telling people that "no matter where they have been, what they have done, who they are sleeping with, what they are smoking or drinking, the lies they have told or the people they have hurt, they should run to Jesus because Jesus will accept and love them" is a dangerous idea. Of course, these people are right. The fact is, I have taken advantage of that message more often than I like to admit, but that is the point. When I do, Jesus still loves me. Is that dangerous? Of course, it is! But, in fact, it is the only idea Christians have worth dink.

If Christians want to communicate truth to those who do not want to hear, it is very important that they lead with Jesus and let the devil take the hindmost. Why is that?

Allowing Jesus to Do the Hugging

Jesus does the hugging, and he hugs some really weird, needy, and sinful people who do not appear to be getting better. In John 21, the resurrected Christ asks Peter three times if Peter loved him; Peter, you will remember, had denied Jesus three times. Then Jesus sends him to the sheep of his pasture. It was Jesus's love that made the conversation relevant.

When I was a young pastor in the Boston area, I attended a meeting of some of the religious leaders. I remember a young man who said that he was a Christian and a Communist. Given the atheistic base of communism, that was a major disconnect to me. I usually manage to keep a straight face when I am playing poker, but hardly in any other place and certainly not in the face of this man's comment. The young man asked me if that bothered me, and I granted that it did. Even more than that, it confused me. Then he asked me a question that I have thought about fairly often since he asked it: "Steve, I'm your brother. If there was ever a war and both of us were in it on different sides, would you kill me?"

That's a good question, and it brings other questions to mind: If I am your brother or sister and am a Democrat (or Republican), will you reject me? If I am gay, and I am your brother, will you reject me? Or if I am your brother and your sister, and my gender has changed, will you reject me? If I am a Calvinist (or Arminian, Dispensationalist, Catholic, Pentecostal, Baptist, etc.), and I am your sister or brother, will you reject me? For the purposes of this book, the question is a bit broader: I am afraid, lonely, sinful, angry, hateful, condemning, but a person for whom you say Christ died. Will you reject me?

The issue is not how Christians define truth, itemize what true Christians believe, or set theological or doctrinal walls around faith. On occasion, those are things that Christians ought to do. But above all, the issue is Jesus, whom he hugs. Frankly, Jesus hugs a lot of weird people I would not hug. He has hugged all believers, and it is reasonable to expect that he will hug others who aren't now a part of our family. He hugged me, and I am not even sure why.

Allowing Jesus to Do the Teaching

Jesus does the teaching, too. In John 13:13 Jesus said that people called him "Teacher" and then said, "you are right, for so I am." Jesus teaches throughout the Gospels. Sometimes, Jesus withholds truth; sometimes, he speaks truth that is widely accepted by his students; at other times, his teaching is so offensive that his students run away. He is helpful, wise, clear—and sometimes, as John R. Stott says, a controversialist.[1] In all of Jesus's teaching, the most salient thing is that what Jesus says is exactly what is needed at exactly the right time.

He is still the Teacher.

I remember a small group Bible study when a man asked for prayer for a new Christian. He was concerned because the young man was moving to another city to attend a university. "I worry so much," he said, "about him and the forces that will challenge his baby faith." Someone in that small group spoke great wisdom and truth, "You shouldn't worry so much about him. He belongs to Jesus, and Jesus has a tender place in his heart for children . . . the physical ones and the spiritual ones. You can trust him."

If you are a Christian, you know that in Christian circles there is a lot of talk about discipleship. We make it a verb, challenging people to disciple others, while we suggest that discipling is the most important and least practiced effort in the church. I have to be careful here because almost everybody I know and respect says that, and when you are the only person who holds a view, chances are you are not a prophet . . . you are just wrong.

However, with that being said, the whole idea of discipling scares the spit out of me because I fear that the process can so easily degenerate into making others like me. Do not get me wrong, the teaching call of the church to present biblical truth to its members is important, but to be honest, my discipling of others calls to mind the horror of "little Steves" sitting in the pews of the church. I do not want that, and you should not either.

I have a fairly extensive prayer list, and each morning I pray for a number of people. When I have time, I have found a new way to pray for those people. Instead of naming my friend and family's needs to a God who cares and already knows those needs, I imagine myself in a church where Jesus is standing in front where there is normally an altar. I picture the people for whom I pray sitting in the pews. Then, again in my imagination, I walk out to the pews, take the person I am praying for by the hand, walk with him or her to Jesus, and get out of the way. Christians' main responsibility in speaking and living truth to a culture of people who do not want to hear is to get them to Jesus and then get out of the way. We can trust the Teacher.

Allowing Jesus to Do the Defining

From there, Jesus does the defining. Christians do not. Jesus is often counterintuitive about what he says, what he does, and whom he loves. Masters do not wash a slave's feet, religious leaders do not hang out with prostitutes, and religious teachers do not contradict the very tenets of the discipline in which they teach. But Jesus does, and almost everything that one would expect from a messiah is exactly what Jesus refuses to do. So if we are followers of Jesus, it is incumbent on us to let him do the defining—not our religion, our preconceived notions, or our personal proclivities.

My friend Eddie Waxer runs a sports ministry that has literally changed the world. Eddie told me once that he had noticed that hardly any Christian will witness to those above them financially, socially, or spiritually, nor to those who are beneath them—it is only to those they consider their equals to whom they bring the truths of Christ. In other words, instead of allowing Jesus to define, Christians define where they go.

A number of years ago, our ministry did a seminar in Portland, Oregon. For the two-day event we brought support staff, musicians, sound people, and a variety of others to help. On the first night, a man sat in the back row who looked like the genetic mix of The Hulk and Frankenstein. The whole time I was teaching, the man just listened with a very hostile scowl on his face. I can remember intentionally not looking at him while I was teaching because every time I did, I could not help but wince. It was so obvious that when the first night was over, and the staff talked about him, we decided to make sure that this man had not broken in and stolen some of the musical instruments and sound equipment. As I went to sleep that night, I prayed that God would keep the man away the second night. As it often happens, God did not define this man as I had, and the next night the man showed again, sat in the same seat in the back, and looked—if possible—even more intimidating than the first night.

When the event was over, the staff started packing up the equipment and I stood in the front of the auditorium signing books and talking to people. When all of the people I was talking to had left and the staff were all in the back, to my horror I saw that monster of a man walking down the aisle in my direction. My whole life passed before me, and I was sure that I was going to die. Then that man, as he got closer, raised his arms, in an apparent effort to either hit me or strangle me. I closed my eyes, preparing to go to heaven, when his arms encircled me in an unbelievable bear-hug, lifting me off the floor and into the air.

"Brother," he said in a low and pretty threatening voice, "I love you, dude. I love your ministry, and from now on I'm going to support what you do financially."

Jesus gets to decide and define who, what, when, and where. His story, love, and presence precede and define every Christian message believers speak.

Allowing Jesus to Do the Maintenance Work

There is one more area of Jesus's job description (the one he wrote himself). Jesus not only does the hugging, teaching, and defining. Jesus holds the maintenance contract. All of believers' efforts to get and keep folks into the fold are above their pay grade. In John 10 Jesus calls himself the good shepherd and then defines what he means, "I lay down my life for the sheep.

And I have other sheep that are not of this fold. . . . My Father, who has given them to me, is greater than all, and no one is able to snatch them out of the Father's hand" (vv. 15–16, 29).

I heard a preacher once say that Jesus does not like people to come to heaven alone, "He rejoices when we bring others with us." I like that sentiment, but it is built on a false premise that Christians do the bringing. We do not, never have, and never will. Only Jesus brings people with him, and he does it quite well.

When I was a young pastor in the Boston area, some college students in our church produced an evangelistic film. I do hope that the film was not shown to too many Christians. In the final scene, there was a young man walking to a wall of flames (hell), and the last thing he does before entering hell is to turn to the audience, point his finger, and ask, "Why didn't you tell me?" After I saw that film, I went into my neighborhood and told all my neighbors that I did not want them to go to hell because I had failed to warn them—actually, I didn't really do that. But I did feel horribly guilty. It was false guilt, because getting people to heaven is God's business.

The late Dan Cole illustrated Jesus's job on his radio show with Moody Broadcasting. One of the pastoral things he would do on air was to provide biblical answers to questions. I did not hear it, but I was told that one time a boy called him and asked Pastor Cole if his recently deceased pet dog would be in heaven. "I don't know, son," Cole said, "When you get there, whistle and see if he comes." That is funny, but there is a profound truth in it, too. Believers are not responsible for anybody else's salvation (certainly not that of their pet), and they are not responsible for anybody being lost for eternity. Frankly, if heaven and hell were dependent on human faithfulness or lack of it, it would be a burden that no Christian could stand. So, when we Christians get to heaven, whistle and look around. We might be surprised.

CHAPTER 6

When Being Right Is
Not Nearly Enough

The scribes and the Pharisees sit on Moses' seat, so practice and observe whatever they tell you—but not what they do. (Matthew 23:2–3)

Effectively speaking and living truth to people who do not want to hear or see is mostly a matter of attitude—not knowledge, planning, training, and technique. If this were a real how-to book, I would give readers a list and make it a part of a system. I am not going to do that, because attitude cannot be systemized.

Later, I will spend a little time on methodology, but here is the meat: I already told you that Christians are right. That is good except for one thing—being right is extremely dangerous for a Christian and, in fact, may be the most destructive danger a Christian ever faces in communicating to those who do not want to hear.

In Matthew 23, Jesus said that the scribes and Pharisees were right because they sat on Moses' seat. Then for nearly the rest of the chapter, Jesus says some of the harshest things he ever said about anybody. The scribes and Pharisees were right, but they were wrong. Jesus called them hypocrites and whitewashed tombs filled with decaying bones. The scribes and Pharisees put heavy burdens on people but would not lift a finger to help. Jesus said the scribes and Pharisees would do almost anything to win a convert, and then make the convert twice the child of the devil than he or she was before conversion.

Jesus said more, but I do not want to talk about it. Do you know why? Because Jesus is not just talking about them—he is talking about us. The Pharisees were the closest thing there was in first-century Judaism to the orthodox, evangelical Christians of today. They really were right about things like biblical authority, the supernatural, angels, miracles, and life after death. Other theological positions in first-century Judaism—e.g., the Sadducees—were wrong on almost all of those points. Why in the world was Jesus so hard on the Pharisees, given that they were mostly right? Jesus knew that being right could make people mean. If the Pharisees were not so close to God's truth, Jesus would have left them alone. They were so close and, at the same time, so very far.

Before I write anything else, it is important to start with a central truth. This particular truth sounds controversial, but it really is not: being Christian has very little to do with getting doctrinal propositions right.

I have a pastor friend who left the denomination of which I am a part, and the church voted overwhelmingly to follow him. I love my friend; in fact, his wife had come to Christ years before at a church where I was the pastor. I called my friend and, among other things, asked him if he still believed in The Westminster Confession (the doctrinal standard of the denomination he left). "Of course I do," he said. "It's just irrelevant."

What did he mean by saying that the confession was true but irrelevant? He did not mean that truth is irrelevant, or that the central truths of the Christian faith are not important. He meant that so often Christians forget that they do not live on truth. It will not keep people warm at night; they cannot eat it when they are hungry; and no matter how much they love truth, truth will not love them back. A Christian lives by that to which the truth points.

I love and value The Westminster Confession of Faith. It is my heritage, and again I believe it to be one of the most profound statements of the Christian faith ever written. But someone needs to write a companion confession outlining the practical implications of the doctrinal propositions. One is orthodoxy, and the other is orthopraxy. The first is the doctrinal truth, the second is how that truth works out in life. Both are important.

Orthopraxy, of course, includes obedience to God's law and faithfulness to his calling. But it also includes the awareness that obedience is often lacking, and that faithfulness sometimes leaves a lot to be desired. It includes being honest about sin and blushing. Orthopraxy includes righteousness, but it also includes forgiveness and mercy. Orthopraxy recognizes sin and calls it what it is, but it also recognizes the pain of the sinner, the failed efforts at obedience, and the power of temptation. Orthodoxy speaks the name of a holy God whose law is perfect. But Christian orthopraxy also speaks the name of *the* God, Jesus, a God of redemption and mercy.

That means Christians really are in this difficult life together, and that the struggle is universal. The struggle does not stop at the church door. Being a Christian really does have less to do with getting doctrine right than one would suppose. Being right is simply not enough.

Does that shock you? It should not. The Scripture says that believing is no big deal, because even demons are believers in truth (James 2:19). They are not that happy with it, but they do believe it. Some of the meanest, most condemning, and most arrogant pains in the posterior I know are right about truth. I know because I have often been that person. And too, some of the kindest, most compassionate and loving Christians I know are so muddled on biblical truth that I sometimes think they are reading a different Bible. I know because I have often been that person, too.

There are some very specific dangers in being right, but it is important to examine a seminal biblical truth about human beings first. Somehow, believers have gotten the idea that before becoming Christians we were lost, flawed, afraid, sinful, and needy folks who, after becoming Christians, got fixed. If you believe that, you will believe anything. You also have not spent much time in the Bible or with Christians.

Every once in a while, some sociological institution reveals that the people in the church have about as many divorces as those outside the church, break the traffic and tax laws at about the same rate as unbelievers, and suffer from depression and anxiety just like everybody else. When those surveys come out, Christian leaders point to them and call for repentance and radical change.

However, the proper response should be "duh!" The fact is, not only are Christians not much better than pagans, they are sometimes a lot worse. The Christian faith is about forgiveness. It is not a moral improvement society. The Christian faith is about a relationship with God and a relationship instituted by God himself. Believers get confused because God's choices and actions often appear irrational. It is insane that God likes me so much; nevertheless, he does.

I am a preacher, seminary professor, media Bible teacher, and author of religious books. I remember telling God what I had discovered about how I thought I would be a lot better by now and adding that, if he really loved me, I would be. His response was laughter and a sigh of relief. He was not shocked. To the contrary, God said, "Finally. Now let's see what we can do with the truth you've discovered."

Being Right and the Danger of Self-Righteousness

The first and mother of all dangers in being right is obviously self-righteousness. God and people can put up with almost anything except self-righteousness. Well, God does put up with it, but it is because of Jesus. Still, I suspect, self-righteousness is irritating to him, and it is certainly irritating to everybody else.

Jesus told a story about the church elder who went to church to pray and was horrified to find that a drunk arrived there before him. I'm changing the details a bit, but the general story is found in Luke 18. The elder prayed (and he knew how to pray) a prayer of thankfulness to God. That was fine until he started listing that for which he was thankful. He told God that he was thankful that he was not like some other people he knew and—looking down his nose at the drunk and wincing at the smell—added, "like that drunk there, for instance." The drunk, on the other hand, said his prayer, "I'm screwed. If you don't have mercy on me, I don't have a prayer."

Then Jesus gave a surprising end to the story: Instead of saying that the drunk roasted in hell, he said that God hugged the drunk, and did not even tell him to stop drinking. On the other hand, Jesus made it clear that God was shocked and offended by the elder's prayer.

God is never shocked when people are not righteous. God never says, "I had such high hopes for you." God does not have perspiration on his forehead over people's failing struggle to get better. He knows and has always known all of that. Instead, God sent his Son to die for all of that, so believers could be justified in his presence. Do you know what causes God to blush? Needy sinners with secrets nobody but God knows, pretending to be righteous and pure. That's what makes God blush.

Is it possible to be right without being self-righteous? It is very difficult, but it is possible some of the time. The late Calvin Miller, in his story about apple thieves, tells about Cora and her new priest, both given to stealing apples. In his self-righteousness, her former priest kicked Cora out of the confessional. Miller writes, "After Cora and the priest had eaten many a pie, they found they actually were beginning to help each other for support and prayed for each other, and finally both were able to quit stealing apples—*at least they did not steal them all that often. Still, some sins are hard to quit and confirmed apple thieves must help each other pass the best orchards.*"[1] Self-righteousness is sometimes hard to quit, too. Confirmed Pharisees have to help each other speak the truth.

There is an ancillary danger to self-righteousness: Self-righteousness is maybe the only sin that, by its very nature, denies the reality of its own existence. Self-righteousness often wears the mask of piety, compassion, concern, and love. It is the emperor-has-no-clothes sin that requires that others point it out (which, by the way, is hard to do without being self-righteous). Self-righteous people hardly ever know they are self-righteous, and good people rarely ever know they are good.

On occasion God allows believers to see their growth so they will not be discouraged, but he knows that it will go to their head if they take that growth too seriously. On the other hand, because he loves them, he allows believers to see the glass house in which they live, makes knowledge of their sin a gift, and regularly puts them in embarrassingly uncomfortable places where they can see who they really are—sinners saved by faith alone, Christ alone, and grace alone. When Christians understand that as more than just a doctrine but as an existential reality, a wonderful and surprising thing happens—they notice that people are listening when they speak truth.

Being Right and the Danger of Hypocrisy

Another great danger in being right is self-righteousness' ugly sister, hypocrisy. By definition, hypocrisy occurs when Christians say that they believe one thing yet act in a manner contrary to their stated beliefs. Given what I have written about the Bible's teaching on human nature, when a Christian behaves poorly, that is not being hypocritical. In fact, the least hypocritical Christian is probably the worst person around who is not overly concerned that people know it. That is a demonstration of truth, not a violation of it. The pretending is the problem.

In 1521 Martin Luther, in a letter to his rather uptight friend and colleague Melanchthon, wrote, "Love God and sin boldly." That is a well-known quote but there is more to it than just that statement. Here's the full quote, "Be a sinner, and let your sins be strong, but let your trust in Christ be stronger, and rejoice in Christ who is the victor over sin, death, and the world."[2] Christians avoid hypocrisy not by pretending to be good, but by facing the fact that they are not.

Righteous acts are a powerful witness to the truth believers speak, but those righteous acts should never give anyone the impression that Christians are good people doing good because that is what good people do. If we communicate that, it will only cause those who hear to think that the Christian faith is only for good people. And, I might add, those who know us will wince at the duplicity of our witness. Martin Luther said, "The works of the righteous would be mortal sins if they would not be feared as mortal sins by the righteous themselves out of pious fear of God."[3]

I once heard a preacher rail against the sins of his congregation and then, to my great surprise, in the middle of his condemnation, started weeping and said, "I'm so sorry. God just revealed to me that I'm guiltier of what I just said—far more guilty—than anybody in this congregation." I do not know if there were any unbelievers in the church that morning, but I hope there were.

Being Right and the Danger of Selectivity

Another great danger of being right is the problem of selectivity. Someone has suggested that a good practice for

Christians is to read the passages in Scripture that they did not underline. Believers have a tendency to underline only what feeds their own proclivities, affirms their righteousness, and confirms their theological particulars. Jesus referenced this problem in John 5 when he said that the religious folks spent a lot of time searching the Scriptures for eternal life but had missed him.

Selectively communicating truth can be dangerous. I have a friend who says that you often hear fat preachers yelling at gay people, but rarely hear gay people yelling at fat preachers. That has some truth to it, because you and I both know that in some circles sexual sin is condemned while the sin of gluttony gets a pass. However, that is not to assume that the gay community does not do their selective yelling, too. People have their most favorite sins and their least favorite sins, and we are all willing to condemn others on the basis of that understanding.

For instance, I am a teetotaler. In fact, I have never consumed adult alcoholic beverages—ever. I would like to attribute that to my purity, but the truth is that I just cannot get the stuff down. I think, but I am not sure, that God, knowing that almost all the males in my family line are or were drunks, gave me an inability to consume alcohol in order to break the family curse. It probably would be unseemly, given what I do for a living, for me to be a drunk. God fixed it so all wine tastes to me like Kool-Aid gone bad, and Guinness has the consistency and taste of (I imagine) axle grease. In the past, I have talked very negatively about Christians drinking alcohol. I stopped when someone pointed out that I probably ought to keep my views of booze to myself until I stopped smoking my pipe.

Christians have to speak truth about what is and what is not sin. However, people will stop listening (and rightly so) when they see how selective their list is. Racists who do not smoke pot, misogynists who do not gossip, and liars who do not cheat, must speak quietly about pot, gossip, and cheating. Believers can substitute their own sin here. When one thinks,

"I may bad but at least I'm not as bad as . . . " it is dangerous territory.

Being Right and the Danger of Deflection

Another danger of being right is the danger of self-righteousness becoming a deflection. Jesus, in a colorful analogy (Matthew 7), asked why someone would point out the splinter in someone else's eye when they have a log in their own. He went on to suggest that it would be a good idea to get the log out of one's own eye before trying to remove the splinter in someone else's eye. Jesus called it hypocrisy. It is also deflection. It is an effort to keep others from focusing on the log.

Do you remember when Jesus dealt with the woman caught in adultery (John 8)? You will remember that she was about to be stoned by the crowd. John says that Jesus stooped down and wrote something in the dirt. John does not tell us what Jesus wrote, but I think I know. He started describing particular "logs," and after he named each one he looked up at that particular person in the crowd and asked, "Really?" The man then dropped his stone and walked away, thinking better of throwing his stone at the adulterous woman.

Jesus still looks at his own when we manifest our arrogance, judgment, and purity. And he always asks, "Really?" I do not know about you, but that is enough for me. I cannot tell you how often I have dropped my stone and walked away. It is in the act of dropping stones that people who did not want to hear truth begin to ask questions. They might even listen to our truth.

Being Right and the Danger of Confusion

Paul asks some rhetorical questions in Romans 11:34–35, "For who has known the mind of the Lord, or who has been his counselor? Or who has given a gift to him that he might be repaid?" The proper answer to those questions is, "Nobody here." Yet Christians really do think they know the mind of the Lord; they really dare to give God advice, and they really think that God owes them. It is an attitude that suggests that the people of God have the answers to all the questions being asked. The truth is that Christians often do not have the foggiest—and they know it. A bit of humility would be in order.

The history of Christianity is rife with wars—divisions over and persecution by people who were sure they were right and others were wrong. Sometimes they were right, but from God's standpoint, they were all wrong. A significant part of being a Christian is being confused. In effect, Calvin called the Bible, "God's baby talk,"[4] and he was right. For an infinite God to communicate any truth to finite minds, there is the necessity for God to keep the fodder down low, or people would never be able to see any truth. But that does not mean believers know all truth, understand the mysteries (the "secret things" of Deuteronomy 29:29), or have a handle on the explanations. Not even close. My friend and late mentor Fred Smith used to say that the essence of being a mature Christian was to have a high tolerance for ambiguity. Confusion and the necessary and attendant trait of admitting it are powerful communication tools.

Does that mean believers do not have any answers to any questions, can never be sure about anything, or do not understand what has been revealed? Of course not. The verities of the Christian faith are precious truths. But confusion is one of the verities (as in, God is sovereign and we are not). In that sense, confusion becomes a gift when believers recognize it and affirm its existence in them.

I cannot tell how many times I have stood before the grave of a child, cleaned up after a suicide, or told a terminal patient the truth. I had no answers to the questions that were asked. I had only tears. Those tears became a key to the communication. And my confusion became an open invitation to say more about a confusing but loving God.

CHAPTER 7

You Too?

And the Word became flesh and dwelt among us . . .
full of grace and truth. (John 1:14)

There are a number of beliefs and doctrines that make the
Christian faith different from other religious philosophies. I
do not know any religionist (including Buddhists) who would
seriously suggest that all religions are the same.

In the discussion of attitude, there is no more important attitude than identification. In fact, of all the ways the
Christian faith is different, this is at the center. The Creator
has identified with his creatures. Now that really is different,
and it makes everything else different. When the Scripture tells
believers, "Have this mind among yourselves, which is yours
in Christ Jesus, who, though he was in the form of God, did
not count equality with God a thing to be grasped, but made
himself nothing, taking the form of a servant, being born in the
likeness of men" (Philippians 2:5–7), it is giving a significant
key for reaching the world.

So Christians are to be like Jesus, right? Wrong. Or at
least wrong in that many think it means being good and pure,

working miracles, and being nice. Instead, it is about attitude. Having the mind of Christ is an attitude of identification with Christ and with those who are outsiders, in the same way Christ identified with his Father and with outsiders.

Jesus lived, said, and taught everything his Father wanted him to live, say, and teach. I do not know about you, but I cannot pull that off. Jesus's identification with believers is, in essence, different than their identification with others. However, Jesus did do amazing things. He so identified with the drunks and sinners that he was called out for being one of them. Jesus experienced fear (real fear), doubt (real doubt), weariness (real weariness), hunger and thirst (real hunger and thirst), and wondering (real wondering). The incarnation of God in Christ was not a game. The Scripture says he can sympathize with weaknesses because "in every respect [he] has been tempted as we are" (Hebrews 4:15).

The impact of the incarnation of God in Christ was not in Jesus's teaching (other than, of course, in his death and resurrection, and all that accomplished). Almost everything Jesus taught could be found in one form or another in the teaching of the Old Testament. The impact of the incarnation was not in Jesus's example. Human depravity is universal; but with that provision, there were a lot of good, faithful heroes in the Old Testament whom God could have used as examples. The impact of the incarnation was not in Jesus's miracles either. Every one of the miracles Jesus performed is matched (and sometimes surpassed) in the Old Testament. So what is the impact of the incarnation of God in Christ? The impact of the incarnation of God in Christ is the incarnation of God in Christ. It is the amazing, mystifying, incredible, and unbelievable fact that God would identify with humankind.

Jesus told his disciples that he was sending them just as the Father had sent him, but there is a difference. Jesus sympathized with his followers' weaknesses and could identify with them because he was temped just as they were. Believers are sent to sympathize with others' weaknesses because we have been tempted just as they are and have yielded to the temptations in the same way others have. Jesus identified with weaknesses from his strength. A Christian's identification is from weakness with weakness.

Identification with Sin and Weakness

If Christians want to speak and live truth to those who do not want to see it and hear it, the first place of identification is with their sin and weakness. That sounds like a violation of everything the Christian faith teaches, but it is not. It is at the heart of the only witness believers have.

Paul makes an oft-quoted and rarely believed statement in 2 Corinthians 12. Something was wrong with Paul that made him weak—a "thorn in the flesh." Paul pleaded with God to remove his problem. God absolutely refused, and then said to Paul, "My grace is sufficient for you, for my power is made perfect in weakness" (2 Corinthians 12:9). Then Paul said, "shut my mouth." Well, not that exactly. Paul said that he would accept his weakness because "when I am weak, then I am strong" (2 Corinthians 12:10).

I have always looked for a hero I could admire and try to follow. I still do sometimes. I know me, my need and sin, and I have always thought that there were those who knew more than I did, lived the faith far better than I lived it, and who knew God in a deeper and more profound way than I do. Actually, there are a lot of folks who fit that bill. The problem is that when I start building an altar to them, I find out the dirt. I even find out sometimes (not often, but sometimes) that I know better, live better, and know God more than they do.

I remember the first time I found a Christian hero. He was a well-known Christian. One time at lunch he said to me, "Steve, you think way too highly of me, and that's dangerous. So I want to tell you a bit about the dark side." Then because he loved me, this man told me his sins. He did not tell me about stealing a quarter from his mother when he was a little boy or about a white lie he told to a teacher. He told me about real struggles and some significant areas where he had failed. I was shocked. I didn't know what to say. "You thought," he said, "that Jesus didn't have to die for me too?" There have been many heroes after that one, and always with similar results.

After I got over my shock, do you know what happened? This man and I became friends, and I do not have a friend I love more. The relationship does not have anything to do with hero worship or wishing I could be like him (well, okay, maybe I do envy some things; he is better looking and has more money). The relationship is deep, trusting, and honest. When he talks, I listen; if he tried to sell me a used car, I would buy it.

What happened? Identification happened. Instead of a reaction of "I wish" or "I worship," it is now, "You too?" The people we want to see and hear the truth that we live and know will not until we as believers say, "You too?"

Am I suggesting that Christians confess their deepest and darkest secrets to the town gossip or the village atheist? Of course not. But if atheists do not know that believers have deep and dark secrets, we are living a lie. It is no wonder nobody wants to hear the truth we speak.

Identification with Need

Identification includes identification in areas of need, fear, weakness, and anxiety. Jared Wilson has a wonderful book, *The Imperfect Disciple: Grace for People Who Can't Get Their Act Together.* Jared said that he dreaded doing church things because he was not the Christian everybody thought he was. He was afraid of being the kind of Christian they had to let in just because he prayed the sinner's prayer, so he worked hard at faking it. In fact, Jared was a very needy and frightened disciple of Christ and wrote, "It's a wonder I'm not cowering in a corner as I type this very paragraph." He could not blame the church or other Christians for his dysfunctions because he knew "plenty of friends and family who were confident, self-assured, highly functional, perfectly happy people (those jerks) . . . The blame lies deep inside myself. I was born a spiritually dysfunctional person. I grew up kind of neurotic and fearful."[1]

The amazing thing about that kind of statement (and the book is full of similar kinds of personal honesty) is the one who made it. Jared Wilson is a well-known Christian leader, the author of several best-selling books, and a Christian magazine editor. Frankly, people like that do not say things like that. But that is the point. There are certain things Christians do not say publicly. And yet, the Scripture says that God "knows our frame; he remembers that we are dust" (Psalm 103:14), and that he will not break a bruised reed (Isaiah 42:3).

Why not just admit it? Some people will, of course, demean believers because of their weakness, laugh at their failure, and turn away because of their need. But most people, believe it or not, will instead say, "You too?"

Identification with Doubt

There is also the identification of doubt.

A number of years ago Os Guinness wrote a book, *Doubt: Faith in Two Minds*. In it, Guinness pointed out two kinds of doubt—one just plain unbelief and the other something most believers experience. That is the doubt of the father—whose son was mute with a demonic spirit—who said to Jesus, "I believe; help my unbelief!" (Mark 9:24). Guinness wrote that how believers deal with doubt is largely a reflection of the health of their faith, "Find out how seriously a believer takes his doubts and you have the index of how seriously he takes his faith."[2]

The problem is that many Christians (myself included, on occasion) give the impression that we do not have doubts, never wonder, and have no questions. If believers give that impression, they are simply kidding themselves and, thus, giving a false witness to everybody else. Of course Christians have doubts. We believe in a lot of things that—were it not for the supernatural intervention of a supernatural God—would be insane. "Jews demand signs and Greeks seek wisdom" (1 Corinthians 1:22). They still do, and sometimes faith seems quite foolish.

I have been walking with Jesus for a whole lot of years, and the outright doubts that I have had are largely in the rearview mirror. However, every time a baby dies, a woman is abused, a terrorist kills, an earthquake or tornado devastates a town, a father commits suicide, or cancer claims another victim, I wonder, ask the painful questions, and struggle with the doubts. I understand what C. H. Spurgeon meant when he said that God was too good to be cruel, too wise to be wrong, and that when he did not have answers, he should trust God's heart. By and large, that is what I do. But sometimes it is really, really hard.

Not too long ago, I was with some people who were going through a very difficult tragedy. I was asked where God was in all of the pain. For once, I did not give the stock answers. Over the years, I have learned a lot of stock answers that can win debates and impress people, but the problem is that they do not help much with a broken heart. "I wish I knew," I said. One of my friends who was there and not a believer was incredulous, and said, "You too?" We have become friends. He is seriously considering the Christian faith and is not far from the kingdom.

If he had been looking for a debate, I would have won it. But after the debate, I would have never seen him again. There is a place for debate. Christian apologetics (the defense of Christian truth) is sometimes one of God's useful tools—but not very often. Honesty about doubts is almost always better.

If Christians identified with the humanness of life, if we were honest about our doubts, and if made our questions the stuff of our witness, there would be those who would think that we were fools or unsophisticated. Most would say, "You too?" That would be the beginning of a conversation. And who knows where that would lead?

Identification with the Normal

Contrary to some crazy stuff accepted as holy writ in some circles, Christians want (with maybe some exceptions) what everybody wants, they like what everybody likes, and they have desires similar to everybody else's desires. In fact, because of the supernatural in their lives, believers want more. I'm not sure when Christians started denying that their desires are human, and in a whole lot of cases normal and good. So often they have the neurotic feeling that anything one enjoys must be sin and if one did not enjoy it, there is no way it could be sin. That is crazy.

Of course, believers knew it was crazy, but just did not tell one another. Instead of going to those horrible movies, listening to the sinful music, or reading those pagan books, they watched the videos at home with the blinds drawn, played the music when nobody could hear, and kept the books in plain paper wrappers. In the old days, Christians called those movies, music, and books sinful. Now believers say they are idols (it sounds more theologically sophisticated), but it is still crazy. I cannot tell you how many times Christian friends have given up the idol of golf, the idol of food, the idol of clothing, the idol of music, or the idol of recreation, and blamed it on Jesus.

A number of years ago, a major Protestant denomination (in fact, the largest denomination in America) got upset over something Disney did. They called for a nationwide boycott. I assume that millions of Christians quit visiting Disneyland and Disney World. I was kind of glad, given that I am not a Disney fan. Now, I did not have to go and could blame it on Jesus. On the other hand, if my grandchildren forced me to go, at least the crowds would be smaller.

At any rate, during that nationwide boycott of Disney, I went to Disney World with my family. I figured I was safe because no Christians would be there, and no one would know. I do, after all, work for a ministry that is dependent on financial contributions from Christians, and I do have to eat.

Boy, was I wrong.

I cannot tell you how often I ran into Christians that day at Disney World and how often I heard, "Steve? What are you doing here?" I told them that we had a standoff, and I would keep my mouth shut if they did. But I also ran into friends who were not Christians who were also surprised that we were there. They did not say anything, but I could see it in their eyes. They were puzzled. Even though they did not say so, they were thinking, "You too?"

Repeated studies show that Christians and unbelievers really do enjoy the same television programs, music, and movies. We shop at the same stores. We use the same technology, go to the same hairdressers or barbers, exercise at the same places, cry over the same kinds of tragedies, worry about the same financial problems, laugh at the same jokes, and enjoy the same foods as everybody else. Yes, we are to be different (1 Peter 2:9), but by and large, the difference is far deeper than what Christians sometimes call idols. Christians are different because of the way they love the unlovely, forgive the unforgivable, and care for those about whom nobody else cares. What if believers joined the conversation about pop culture and fads, went to the neighborhood cookout without looking down their noses at the beer, and surprised their acquaintances by inviting them to a concert that was not Christian music?

Unbelievers might not say it, but they would think it, "You too?!" Christians never know where that could lead.

Identification with Death

There is one more, a final place (pun intended) of identification. It is in the universal experience of death and the concomitant fear of it. Do you remember the first time you encountered your own mortality? It may have been during the loss of a loved one, on a battlefield, in escaping a dangerous accident, or at a funeral. Whatever it was, maybe for the first time you came up against the wall of reality that your time was coming.

If you are reading this, and you are young, you know about death. However, death may feel like something that happens to others—old people, those who are not careful, and those who were just unlucky—but not you. Besides, by the time you get there, science will have figured out an escape. Trust the old guy on this—there will come a time when death will become existential, and in the wee hours of the night, it will haunt you. The time will come when the idea of death will be quite real (as in "I'm going to die! Me! What?"). If you are a Christian and have not been there yet, when it happens, do not run from the fear. Run to it. When you get there, you will find a whole lot of others there too, and most of them will not be Christians.

My wife and I went through Hurricane Andrew, the greatest natural hurricane disaster to ever hit America, until Katrina. It was a terrible time. We were in our house with a friend, her cat, and our dog. When the roof went, I saw my life pass before my eyes. Our neighbor who had done everything right—boarded up, taped his windows, brought the lawn furniture inside, and tied down the trusses—seemed safe. We did not have time to do any of that, and in fact drove back from the mountains of North Carolina to face the hurricane with our neighbors. Is that stupid or what?

When it got really bad and the roof was going, I told my wife and our friend that when the eye passed through, we would run across the street and hunker down with our prepared neighbors. The eye passed through and the winds died down, but when we opened the front door preparing to run across the street to our neighbor's house, there was no house. It had been blown away.

That was a scary time, but the next morning, all the neighbors met in the street, in front of our devastated houses. We did not even know many of each other's names, but we had been scared together, prayed together (even the atheist next door), and faced death together. There was an incredible bond that, in some ways, exists today. The reality of death does that. It creates a level playing field.

Have you ever noticed the demeanor of people at funerals? We all know—believers and unbelievers, atheists and preachers—that we are going to die. Death is, believe it or not, a conversation starter and a major place of identification. It was surprising how many of my unbelieving neighbors were open to conversations about God because we had faced death together. We all face death together.

When my late mentor Fred Smith died, I went to Dallas to participate in the funeral. It was a large auditorium with a whole lot of people. Then Fred showed up. Well, not really. But shortly before his death, Fred filmed a video to be played at his service. I did not know he had done that and was quite surprised to look up at the large screen and see Fred grinning down on us. He said, among other things, that with so many people there, it would be a shame not to say something. Fred told his friends who were not Christians that he had loved being friends with them, and they were a major gift in his life. He wanted to say goodbye. Then he said to the believers, "I'll see you later."

That moment was electric! What would happen if believers identified with all the darkness of mortality and said to their friends (after they had earned the right to say it) that they wanted to see them later, and then said a word about Jesus who promised that they would? That would be place of powerful identification.

Who knows? Maybe they would see these friends later.

CHAPTER 8

Love Happens

So now faith, hope, and love abide, these three; but the
greatest of these is love. (1 Corinthians 13:13)

I want to talk to you about love, but it is hard. I have been
putting off writing this chapter—not because I do not have
anything to say. I am a preacher and teacher, and I always
have something to say. I have preached and taught often on
the subject of love. I am not having difficulty in writing this
chapter because I am unloving (even though sometimes I am),
or because I do not think love is a good thing (it is). The difficulty is not because love is not important. In fact, there is no
way believers can speak truth without love, and certainly no
reason to live it before the world except for love. It is not that
it has become such a cliché (even though it has). The difficulty
is not because there is only one word in English for love when
there are several different kinds of love (there are at least four
different words in the Greek). And it is not because I think
everything that can be said about love has already been said
(even though it has).

71

The reason this is a hard chapter to write is because I have discovered that so much of what I have said, taught, and preached about love is either wrong or irrelevant. And so have many Christians.

Believers too often have made love an impossible and unreachable standard of the Christian walk. Christians faked love for so long that, most of the time, they do not even know what it is anymore.

You might already know that the title of this chapter comes from the 2009 film of the same title. The film is about a therapist whose wife is killed in a car accident. He writes a book (it's what I sometimes do, and for the same reason) claiming he wants to help others, but what he's really doing is dealing with his own issues. It's a feel-good, idealistic, and kind of shallow movie, but with a good point. I'll spare you the details, but the therapist is surprised by a number of things. In his efforts to fix others, the therapist discovers that he is the one who needs fixing. Then, to his amazement and joy, love happens.

It does, you know. Love—as is true in a number of important things—is something we very often discover when we're on the road to and looking for somewhere else. You're probably familiar with the popular television show, *Candid Camera* (there have been several versions of the show between 1948–2014). The concept was simple: they created an unusual, funny, or crazy situation and recorded how people reacted to it—with a hidden camera. The show's moniker—said at the end of all of the episodes and even a part of the theme music—was to the effect that when you least expected it, you should smile because "you're on candid camera."

Love happens kind of like that. When you least expect it, you find love in all sorts of surprising places. When it happens, it's God. The Scripture says that God not only loves, is loving and loves us, but that God *is* love (1 John 4:8). That's who God is. It's called an "attribute" of God, meaning that wherever you encounter love, there is a sense in which you encounter

God. It's not something one defines very well, can put in a
gift-wrapped box, or even adequately put in doctrinal form.
At any time, in any place, and when you least expect it, love
really does happen—and when it does, you know it and are
surprised by it.

I have a friend who says that he loves Christmas except for
the Jesus part. When everybody else is trying to put Jesus back
in Christmas, my friend is trying to get him out of it. My friend
loves the parties, food, celebration, gifts, and all the family
things, but Jesus keeps messing it up. I always thought my friend
had a point, but I am not going there. However, love and its central place in the Christian walk and witness is sort of like Jesus
and Christmas. Just as there is always the "What about Jesus?"
part of Christmas, there is always the "What about love?" thing
about the Christian faith.

However, love is also like Jesus at Christmas. There is so
much other stuff that people hardly ever experience it, understand it, or practice it anymore, at least the real thing.

So what should believers do about it?

Nothing. For God's sake, do nothing.

But I am getting ahead of myself.

For years, the ministry with which I am associated (Key
Life Network) conducted a seminar on radical grace titled
"Born Free." I have taught the seminar material in a number of
countries and seminary classrooms. When people heard that it
was a seminar on grace, they immediately thought, *Been there,
done that, got it.* It was like selling ice cubes or air condition-
ing to people who live in the Arctic. A chapter on love could
have the same problem. When any writer, preacher, or teacher
starts talking about love, most Christians think, *Been there,
done that, got it.*

Actually, we believers often do not understand love. Yet,
it is probably the most salient attitude Christians can feel and
practice in their lives, and certainly in their witness. There is
something about love that changes everything. The Scripture

says, "Let love be genuine" (Romans 12:9). What this means is that there is a kind of love that is not genuine. It is so very important that love be the real thing, or the attitude will become just another cliché that nobody understands and therefore nobody experiences. "I love you so much that I don't want you to miss Christ and be lost for all of eternity" (even if it is sincere and well-intended) can become another manipulative tool in the Christian toolbox.

Just a cursory reading of Scripture teaches how central love is to everything. The popular belief that the Old Testament is a book of wrath and the New Testament is a book of love is simply spurious. On the contrary, the loving-kindness of God shouts from every page of the Old Testament. Try reading about the love of God in Hosea 11 or in the Psalms and see if it does not move you deeply. Jesus came because "God so loved the world" (John 3:16), and his unconditional love is the focus of his biblical biographies culminating in the cross—the most astounding act of love in all of human history.

Jesus taught that Christians are defined by love for one another and that the world would know about him because of their love for one another. Jesus said that it was love that would cause the world to notice and understand about him. Paul wrote the amazing "song of love" in 1 Corinthians 13, and nothing before or since has spoken of love with greater beauty and power.

How can a Christian love other Christians (no mean task but the first step), and then, how can a Christian love those who would rather be left alone? If believers are going to love, it is important that we understand what it really is—and it is not what many Christians have mostly thought it was.

I am not so arrogant or naïve to suggest that this chapter is new revelation, or that I will straighten out the spurious teaching extant in the church for thousands of years. I simply want to point out what has always been there.

In 1 Corinthians 13, Paul struggles with the idea of love, and while what Paul writes is incredibly beautiful it is not definitive. Paul is not giving a definition of love but a description of its essence. Paul says that if people have everything and do not have love, they do not have anything important. Love is kind; love is not envious; and love is not prideful. Love affirms others; love does not often get angry; and love is happy about the good, the true, and the beautiful. Love is protecting, trusting, hopeful, and keeps on keeping on. Then Paul says that when everything else is gone, love will still be around.

That is the essence of love, but it will drive people nuts if they use it as a checklist. Almost everything in 1 Corinthians 13 can be faked, and people are all good at that. Do you (or anybody else you know) live without a degree of anger, never envy, never show pride? Do you (or anybody else you know) always trust, always remain hopeful, never give up? Have you (or anybody else you know) always found great happiness in the good, true, and beautiful? Is it not true that people rejoice in what they call justice when someone gets what they deserve? How about kindness, when you are on the receiving end of gossip or slander? The danger of 1 Corinthians 13 (and a great variety of other passages in Scripture about love) is that people can check off the items listed therein and do (at least publicly) what is required, but very often others know when the love is fake. People sense when what is on the inside is quite different than what is on the outside. The truth is that love is an inside job, and there is not a thing—not one single thing—you and I can do to fix the inside.

Sometimes it is helpful to understand something by understanding what it is not.

Love Is Not Just a Verb

Most Bible teachers (myself included, on occasion), for instance, teach that love is not a feeling but an action; love is not a noun but a verb; and love is not what is inside people but what they do on the outside. That sounds good, but it is not true. When love is taught that way, it becomes a prescription for bogus love. Someone tells an old and possibly apocryphal story about a Puritan who proposed marriage to the woman he wanted to marry. "I hope," he wrote, "I have no foolishness called romance. I am too well balanced for that sort of nonsense. But we might look forward to leading useful lives and enjoy the respect of the neighbors." Love? Not even close, even if it is true and right.

In *Fiddler on the Roof*, when Tevye asks his wife Golde if she loves him, she sings that for twenty-five years she has washed his clothes, cooked his meals, cleaned his house, given him children, and milked his cow. After twenty-five years she wonders why he is talking about love. Tevye knows all of that, but there is something else he is asking, something more. He wants to know why she did all of that. Love is more than a verb, or it is not love. Love is more about feelings and passions than it is about actions. Actions reflect love, but they are not love. Love just happens.

Love Is Not Useful

Love is not useful. The danger of writing about love is the danger of seeing love as a tool to get people who are not altogether happy with the Christian faith to listen. When love becomes utilitarian it is not love because there is no reason or purpose for love except love itself. In Brennan Manning's book *The Relentless Tenderness of Jesus*, he quotes from the play *Gideon* by Paddy Chayefsky. Gideon is angry with God and goes out into the desert where God comes and overwhelms Gideon with his love. Gideon asks God to tell him that he loves him. God replies that he does. Then Gideon asks God, "God, why do you love me?" There is a long silence, and then God responds, "I really don't know . . . sometimes my passion is unreasonable."[1] God's passion really is unreasonable, and so is ours. Love just happens.

Love Cannot Be Controlled

Love cannot be controlled, grasped, and bottled up in order to keep it. When I was growing up in the mountains of North Carolina, one of my favorite evening pastimes was to catch fireflies. Sometimes I would catch a lot of them, carefully putting them in a mason jar and creating a kind of lamp. I learned to set the fireflies free before going to bed because if I did not, the next morning they would all be dead. Love is like that.

One of the tragic things about failed marriages is that very often couples expect from their spouse that which no one person can give. In other words, they think and often say, "It's us against the world, and we're all that we need." Then in an effort to make that spurious assumption work, those couples will withdraw from friends, relationships, and normal social networks. Then like those fireflies, the love that was exclusive begins to die. Love cannot be controlled and held tightly. When that happens, love vanishes.

Love Cannot Be Manufactured

Love cannot be manufactured. No matter what anybody says, love is not like a faucet people can turn on and off at will. There are not five steps on how to love. It just does not work that way. I once told a man that he should bring flowers to his wife at least once a week and say that he loved her at least five times a day. I repented when she called me and said, "Steve, will you tell my husband to stop it? He's driving me crazy. When he brings me flowers, I get the feeling he's screwing around; and when he says that he loves me it's like he's checking off something on his to-do list."

Telling unloving people that they should love is the equivalent of telling people who are drowning that if they would just swim, they would be fine. If they could swim, they would not be drowning. Love is like that. There are a lot of sermons on love (I have preached them on occasion) that suggest that if people are not loving, they should stop being unloving and just

77

love. I wish sermons like that were powerful, but they are not. No one can talk anyone into loving or tell them to manufacture it. Love just happens.

Love Is Not Often Recognized

Love is not often recognized. Most of the people who love and are loved do not recognize that they love or are loved. Such affection is almost always a secondary discovery with a "wow" attached to it. In the conversation between Tevye and Golde from *Fiddler on the Roof*, the audience at the movie or play almost always laughs at what Golde says to Tevye, and then as the song progresses, something changes. People become very quiet, and some even get out their handkerchiefs to wipe tears from their eyes. That is when people begin to feel the love they first overlooked. Love happened.

Love Cannot Be Earned

Love cannot be earned. People sometimes confuse love and reward, and they are not even close to being the same. When I was in seminary and studying pastoral psychology, I studied the work of Karen Horney, a German psychoanalyst who in the last part of her career practiced in the United States and questioned some of the major teachings of Sigmund Freud. Horney illustrated love by saying that there was "father love" and then there was "mother love." Father love says, "I'll love you as long as you do what pleases me." On the other hand, mother love says, "I'll love you no matter what." Aside from the sexist flavor to her comments, she was making an important point. Let me make another important point. Horney was wrong about "father love." There is no such thing. What she describes as "father love" is not love at all. It is reward and manipulation. Love happens, but "father love" does not. It is not love.

What Is Love?

Love is Jesus. That is it. If people go much further in trying to understand love than Jesus, they will miss it. John says:

> So we have come to know and to believe the love that God has for us. God is love, and whoever abides in love abides in God, and God abides in him. By this is love perfected with us, so that we have confidence for the day of judgment, because as he is so also are we in this world. There is no fear in love, but perfect love casts out fear. For fear has to do with punishment, and whoever fears has not been perfected in love. We love because he first loved us. (1 John 4:16–19)

C. S. Lewis referred to lust in one of his science fiction books, and he said that if someone reading what he wrote had never experienced an overwhelming sexual lust no description would suffice, but if the reader had experienced it, nothing else needed to be said. That is true of love when it is real. If you have never been loved deeply, without condition, and without requirement, I do not have the words to explain it to you. On the other hand, if you have experienced it, I really do not have to say much more.

A number of years ago, I wrote the book *Three Free Sins*. Its main thrust was that the reason people are so bad is that they are trying so very hard to be good. The trying is often so prideful, ego-centered, and narcissistic that holiness is hardly ever the product. The message of the book was that—because of justification (we're forgiven), imputation (we're clothed in the righteousness of Christ), and adoption (we now have a cool father)—believers can lighten up and allow God to show them his love when they get better and when they do not. And then, Christians will be surprised with the goodness that often follows. That happens because goodness and failure to be good are no longer the issue. Jesus has taken care of that, and now believers can go out and play.

It is the same way with love, being loved, and loving others. Christians have been trying way too hard to love, and the harder they try, the less they love. The more people chase love, the more it recedes. Try to define, manufacture, control, earn, or use love, and love will not be found. But if people give up trying to look for love in all the wrong places, love finds them. And that love will become the key to their efforts to speak and live the truth we've been given. The reason God did not send a book to express his love, but instead sent his Son, was because of the nature of love. Love is not a concept, an action, or a doctrine. Love is an experience, both when it is received and when it is given.

A number of years ago when our oldest granddaughter Christy was little, she was playing with her Madeline doll. She was trying to put clothes on her doll, but it was not working. She became quite frustrated. Her father Jim and I were watching a football game on television, and Jim said to Christy, "Try a little patience, honey, and you'll get it." Do you know what Christy did? She threw Madeline at her father, and when he admonished her, she threw the beanbag chair she was sitting on at him.

"That's it," Jim said, picking her up. "You're going to be in time out and you're going to stay there." As he walked away with Christy on his shoulder, she was saying things like "I hate you!" and "I'm never speaking to you again!" Jim said he was fine with that, put Christy in a chair, and told her not to dare move before he told her to. Then Jim and I went back to watching the football game. Actually, Jim did; I never left because wise grandfathers learn to stay out of those kinds of altercations.

A while later, Christy came slowly back into the family room. She was crying. Christy climbed up onto her father's lap and said, "Daddy, I'm so sorry. I don't know why I do stuff like that. I love you so much." Jim hugged her and said, "And Christy, I love you so much . . . more than you will ever know."

Love happened. Nobody planned it or used it. It just happened.

So if Christian love is the key to reaching a world that does not want to be reached, what do believers do?

Nothing! And above all, do not do anything religious.

Jesus showed love by being love. Jesus hung out with the wrong people, said the wrong things, and hugged those nobody else would hug. And he was quite harsh in what he said to those religious people who violated the essence of their faith by making obedience to a very demanding God the center of their belief system. He called them "whitewashed tombs" and a "brood of vipers," who often took a searcher for God and made him a "child of hell" (Matthew 23:27, 33, 15).

Years ago, I heard Jerry Falwell, Sr. speak to a convention of Jewish rabbis in Miami Beach. A Jewish friend had invited me and, other than Falwell, I was the only Gentile there. I did some serious praying for Jerry Falwell. During the question-and-answer portion of his presentation, a rabbi asked, "Dr. Falwell, what is it exactly that you want from us?"

"I don't want anything from you," Falwell answered. "I don't need anything from you and I'm aware that many of you aren't happy that I'm here. I'm here because I wanted to tell you that I love you and, even if you don't want me to love you, I'm still going to love you. I want you to know that I'm going to be your friend and, even if you don't want me to be your friend, I'm still going to be your friend."

Falwell received a standing ovation.

Christians do not get many standing ovations, as it were. Do you know why? Because our agendas almost always precede and define everything we say and do, and certainly that is true about love. Love often turns into theological demands and religious definitions, or even worse, syrupy and cloying drivel.

What do believers do? Again, nothing.

Well, there *is* something: just let Jesus love you. I am not even sure what that means but it feels like forgiveness, acceptance, and delight. Go back and read 1 Corinthians 13. Instead of reading it as a condemnation of the love you do not have or a definition of what you want, change the words "love is" to "Jesus's love for me is." It does not matter that you are not worthy (and I'm talking to Christians in general here, and to myself in particular), that you have sinned, or that you have a lot of doubts. It does not matter where you have been, what you have done, what you have been smoking or drinking, the shameful secrets you cannot share with anyone, the people you have hurt, the anger you feel, the unfairness you have experienced, the piled-up failures you have, or what people who do not know you think about you. In fact, the most important part of the Christian faith is not church or doing religious things or witnessing or being good. It is simply hanging out with Jesus and experiencing his unconditional and relentless love for you.

Then what? Do not leave. Stay there until everything in this chapter makes sense and becomes a reality in your life. Stay there until you have experienced the love that happens in his presence. It might take a few days or a few years—that is OK.

Then what?

Go mingle and see what happens.

CHAPTER 9

Shock and Awe

. . . but in your hearts honor Christ the Lord as holy, always being prepared to make a defense to anyone who asks you for a reason for the hope that is in you. (1 Peter 3:15)

"Shock and awe" is not just about bombs. It is the nature of a Christian witness to people who have no interest in that witness. I have a friend who told me that I should not use the words "shock and awe" because of the militarist connotations, so I honestly tried to think of a different description. I just could not find a better one. Christians do not use those words to describe their witness for Christ, but maybe it is time they did. For years I have been teaching that Christians should live with such freedom that uptight Christians will doubt their salvation. Christians should do exactly the same thing for unbelievers—shock them and create awe.

Reggie Kidd is the dean of the Cathedral Church of Saint Luke in Orlando, my former seminary colleague, author of the best book I have ever read on worship, and my friend. Reggie once asked his son Charlie if he could go with him to a rock concert. It is an understatement to say that the music was not Reggie's favorite, but his son was far more important to Reggie than his taste in music. Charlie was surprised and delighted that his father wanted to go with him.

When the mostly young people were dancing and jumping to the music, one of Charlie's friends—with black fingernails, purple hair, and in-your-face Goth clothes—asked Charlie who the old guy was. Quite proudly, Charlie said, "That's my father." She turned and walked up to Reggie, and said, "You know what? You are one badass dad!"

I am not suggesting that Christians have to go to music concerts they cannot stand, attend movies that offend them, or drink beer even though they cannot abide the stuff. The details belong to individual Christians. However, I am saying that if Christians are not, on occasion, creating shock and awe, they are probably not doing it right. Let me give some suggestions on ways to live so that unbelievers take notice and ask questions.

Shock and Awe in Speaking Truth

If you want to create some questions in the minds of unbelievers, stop lying. Paul said to the Ephesians that, instead of being tossed and turned by every fad and belief system, they should "Rather, speaking the truth in love, we are to grow up in every way into him who is the head, into Christ" (Ephesians 4:15). Christians do not have to shout and condemn insufferably and self-righteously about truth, but they do need to speak it.

At the skeptics forum I used to conduct, I met with unbelievers on Monday evenings for a number of weeks. They would choose the subjects, and each evening I would spend ten to fifteen minutes talking about what the Bible and Christians thought about a particular subject (e.g., Is the Bible true?

Is Jesus God? What about a good God and evil? Does God exist? What is God like? etc.). Then, for the next two hours, we would debate the issue. Many of those who attended those Skeptics Forums would become Christians, but never as many as one particular evening.

One of my rules for skeptics forum was that no Christians were allowed to attend, except me. I stuck by the rule and only violated it once. That was when my late friend Rusty Anderson asked if he could attend. Rusty was a graduate of Westminster Seminary in Philadelphia—not because he wanted to be a pastor, but because he wanted to know more than his pastor knew. He, in fact, was a successful stockbroker who loved Jesus with all his heart, cussed like a sailor, drank adult beverages with delight, smoked cigars, and was so far out of the box that a lot of people really did doubt his salvation.

I told Rusty he could come to skeptics forum on one condition, "Rusty, you can come if you'll just keep your mouth shut." He agreed and, to my surprise, Rusty was quiet until the third session when all of sudden, in the middle of a very sensitive and quiet discussion with the skeptics, he slammed his fist on the desk and it sounded just like a gunshot. "I'm sick of this," he said. "All you folks are carrying on this discussion like it really doesn't matter. Fact is, if there's a hell, you're going there, and over the last two meetings I've grown quite fond of you. The thought of your being lost for eternity really bothers me. I just don't want to go to heaven if you're not going to be there."

Talk about shock and awe. I thought Rusty had just destroyed the very careful and sensitive case I was building for the Christian faith. Not so. That evening turned out to be one of the best evangelistic successes I ever had at a Skeptics Forum. His blunt honesty opened the door to a lot of the participants coming to Christ.

Sometimes nice and sensitive is nothing more than a desire to be accepted. Christians sometimes compromise the truth and sand it down to make it palatable—so palatable that it is no longer the truth. For God's sake, we believers have got to stop that. Paul said that we should speak the truth in love. It means speaking with an awareness that we are sometimes wrong and that we are not the best examples of the truth we speak. But also, love is never manifested by ignoring truth. Rusty loved those in attendance at the forum by speaking the truth.

Shock and Awe in Confession

Christians can create shock and awe in honest confession. The Scripture says that believers should confess their sins to one another (James 5:16). I assume James was talking confession among Christians, but if you want to shock people and create a degree of awe, do it everywhere you go—when it is appropriate and even sometimes when it is not.

Most people believe—whether they are inside or outside the church, Christian or atheist, or believer or unbeliever—that the church is a place to gather if you are good. Christians and non-Christians do not agree on much, but on that one thing there is pretty general agreement. Of course it is a lie, but there is payout in perpetuating that lie. Believers get to feel good about themselves ("I'm a sinner, but I'm better than 'them'"), and unbelievers get to point out the hypocrisy of Christians ("at least I'm honest"). That payback is self-righteousness. That payout is fine for unbelievers, but it is not for Christians. God will not let us get away with it because it violates the very essence of the Christian faith.

Christians have all been saddened by the public revelation of sins within the church—dishonesty with money, sexual immorality, and Christian con games. With each headline, every Christian has winced, and we should have. But there is an upside to all the negative headlines—the growing disabuse of the lie that people have to be good to be in the church. I do think that if we Christians would confess it before God and expose our sin, it would not be so painful.

What if believers allowed the Scriptures to define what it means to be a Christian? We Christians have mostly allowed our culture to do it for us, but what if we studied the Bible with the astonishment it was written to solicit? The Bible does not paint a very pretty picture of God's covenant people. Early on, God called his people "stiff-necked": "And the LORD said to Moses, 'I have seen this people, and behold, it is a stiff-necked people'" (Exodus 32:9). The rest of the Bible is an illustration of God's observation.

Moses messed up so badly that he was not allowed to go into the Promised Land to which he had led the people. Our covenant forefathers and foremothers were a bunch of liars, con artists, prostitutes, and cheats. One even told a king that his wife was his sister so the king could sleep with her. One of our forefathers ran a con game to get his father's blessing—the blessing that would apply to all of God's people. Then there was David, a murderer and adulterer. Jeremiah tried to get out of serving God because it was so difficult. Peter ("the Rock") was clearly a hypocrite, and Scripture points out that he was a hypocrite years after he had walked with the resurrected Christ (Galatians 2:11–14).

And church fights? The early church makes today's church fights look like love feasts. They were not a group of people who sat around the fire singing "Kumbaya." Two of the most prominent leaders in the early church disliked each other so much that they could not even work together. Paul (the writer of much of the New Testament) had a serious problem with pride, and even when he was bragging and confessed what he was doing, he went on doing it. Paul was clear about God's grace when he wrote, "The saying is trustworthy and deserving of full acceptance, that Christ Jesus came into the world to save sinners, of whom I am [not "used to be"] the foremost" (1 Timothy 1:15).

I do not want to give the wrong impression here because there is a lot more to be said, but even with the good parts, it is really hard to find haloes above the heads of those who belong to God. Jesus was very comfortable with sinners, and that was one of the chief charges against him.

What if it was clear that Christians were not in the church because they were good—and what if believers were the ones who made that clear? There would be a good deal of shock and awe. And not only that, we Christians could at least escape the charge of hypocrisy. Christians are not hypocrites when they do bad things; they are hypocrites when they pretend that they do *not* do bad things. Why is that? It is because the Christian faith clearly teaches that Jesus came for sick people, and Christians only become hypocrites when they pretend to be well.

Shock and Awe in Being Human

Christians create shock and awe when they are human and admit it. Paul said that believers "have this treasure in jars of clay, to show that the surpassing power belongs to God and not to us" (2 Corinthians 4:7). Paul is not talking primarily about sin, but about the fact that we Christians are human.

There is an anecdote about a man who was a patient at a mental hospital. His psychosis was manifested in his belief that he was dead. After a good deal of therapy, he did not get better and continued to affirm that he was dead. A psychiatrist, who had tried everything else, decided to try logic. He got the man to agree with the proposition that dead people do not bleed. Once that agreement was clearly stated and agreed on, the psychiatrist took a pin and pricked the finger of the man who was sure he was dead. He, of course, begin to bleed. The psychiatrist, thinking he had finally solved the man's problem, was quite frustrated when the man said after a long pause, "Well, dead people really do bleed."

Paul says that Christians should "consider" themselves dead (Romans 6:11), and at least in that sense, dead people do bleed. They not only bleed; they get depressed, get spitting angry, cry with frustration, experience loneliness and loss, make bad business decisions, say and believe dumb things, are afraid, and are irrational. Christians are not outsiders of the human race, and when they pretend that they are it causes normal people to turn away.

My wife and I live in central Florida and, as I write this, we just went through Hurricane Irma. We were fortunate this time and did not suffer too much damage. We did lose our power, though, and I did not have coffee for almost three days. Finally, out of frustration, I decided to go out and look for a power company truck. "That repairman doesn't run the company," my wife said. I told her that I would feel better if I could just yell at somebody. I went out twice looking for a truck but without success. My wife said later, "That was because of my prayers."

Does that irrational anger shock you? Consider Paul's angry words are recorded in Scripture, "I wish those who unsettle you would emasculate themselves!" (Galatians 5:12). If you are a preacher, try saying that in the pulpit and see how the church leadership responds. Christians are not some sort of pure and superhuman beings who do not bleed. In fact, I have shared stories about my anger in a sermon to a church with several unbelievers in attendance, and one of them said to me that it was a relief to find a human Christian.

I have a friend, Gregg Malik, who struggled with cancer, went through some horrible times, and eventually died. During the time he was dealing with cancer, Gregg wrote a blog to serve as a witness to his friends. Here is what he shared:

> In our culture we like stories that have a beginning, a middle, and an ending, but in real life, things are not so neat. In a fairytale, Prince Charming marries Sleeping Beauty, and they live happily ever after. That sounds nice to children, but adults know that there is a lot of pain and suffering in life. Beauty fades, old age sets in, health fails and we all die. We like to think that we are

in control of our destiny, but much of what happens in life is beyond our control.

As I write this, my future is uncertain. . . . Something showed up on my latest CT scan that is a cause for concern. I didn't need a doctor to know that something is wrong. In a few days, I'll be checking into the Moffitt Cancer Center to see what they can do for me. At this time, things are uncertain.

Are you wondering what kind of Christian witness that was? Let me tell you. It is the witness of a very human Christian who was struggling. He and his wife Nancy were clinging to Jesus with all they had, but more than that, Gregg's honesty is a powerful testimony to what it means to be human and Christian.

The Christian witness to the world is often how God fixes things—and of course he fixes things, but sometimes he does not. We believers like to proclaim to the rooftops how God has healed cancer, allowed us to win the lottery, beat the socks off the opposing team, grew hair, or made us famous. What if our witness had a different shape? What if the unbelieving world saw the pain and embarrassment that all people experience, and noticed that Christians ran to Jesus instead of a bar? What if they saw human believers who struggled and still proclaimed a God who is good, and good all the time? What kind of witness would that be? That's the kind of thing that destroys our Christian witness, right? Wrong. It is the kind of thing that says to our friends that we are human and that when Jesus found us, we did not stop being human.

Gregg wrote in that same blog:

My human nature does not like uncertainty. I want to know what is going to happen next, so I can plan and prepare. But I think God wants me to be uncertain. . . . Jesus said, "Therefore do not worry about tomorrow, for tomorrow will worry about itself. Each day has enough trouble of its own." This concept is more than just wise teaching, this is becoming real in my life, not by my choice, but by the heavy-handed hammering away by God himself.

Shock and Awe Flowing from Mercy

Christians also create shock and awe when they show mercy in an unmerciful world.

I remember the STEP foundation—presenting the gospel in at-risk communities by elevating people to a better life. "The people of God are here, and we're going to fix it," was their message. They did not fix it—the world does not get fixed until Jesus comes back to fix it—but they made it better. Christians have not been called to fix the world, but we are called to be present, to bring some light and hope, to care when nobody else does, to bind up wounds, to feed hungry people, and to stand for justice for the oppressed. Jeremiah, I would again remind believers, said that God's people were to seek the welfare of the city where they resided (Jeremiah 29:7).

I was once on a radio talk show with an atheist host. He was quite proud of the fact that he and his listeners had raised twenty thousand dollars for the hungry. "Nonsense!" I said. "You don't give a rip about the poor. Christians raise ten times that amount every second of every day. How many hospitals have you built? How many schools have you started? Tell me the ravaged areas of the world where you have gone and stayed until houses were rebuilt, streets cleaned up, and people were safe? You don't have the foggiest idea of what it means to make a difference in a dark world. Christians have been doing it thousands of years before you were born and we still are." I know, that was pretty prideful and arrogant, and I have repented. But frankly it felt good to say it, because it was true.

I have a friend who works for the relief arm of a large Christian denomination. After one of the many national disasters Americans often experience, my friend went to live where the disaster had taken place. He and hundreds of Christian volunteers went about restoring houses. One of the houses destroyed in the disaster was owned by a lesbian couple who were not Christians. One volunteer became insistent that he was not going to work on a home owned by lesbians, for fear of affirming their sin. My friend had a "come to Jesus" talk with the volunteer, explained to him about the people Jesus hung out with (them and us), and the rebuilding work continued.

Many of the Christians became friends with this lesbian couple and, while they did not come to Christ, I suspect they were not far from the kingdom. Let me tell you the rest of the story: my friend and his wife are childless, and it is a difficult place in their lives. One evening, years after the disaster, my friend received a call from his lesbian friends. "We know that you guys have always wanted children and we've thought about it. We want to make an offer to you. We will bear your child." One of the lesbians said that she would be artificially inseminated and that their gift to my friends would be the baby. My friend cannot even tell that story without getting emotional— "shock and awe" on both sides of the Christian aisle.

As Christians, our good works are not necessary to please God (he is already pleased), but they do please and surprise our neighbors. It is important for the neighbors' sakes that they see Christians show up in the darkness. We are not all called to be social workers, but we are commanded to be there even if our presence confuses those we serve. That, of course, is the point.

Shock and Awe When Christians Cut Slack

We live in a world that is quite unforgiving. That is clear in social media—an adequate and even accurate reflection of our culture. I suppose that social media is a good thing in some ways, but it has also created a "gotcha" culture of condemnation, hatred, and division. I am certainly unfamiliar with cussing and spitting, and there is very little I hear that offends my pure heart. . . . Obviously, that is not true. The fact is that my heart is not altogether that pure, and my language is not altogether or always pristine. But today's culture has become such a calloused, angry, offended, and hateful culture that I am even shocked. That is bad.

Actually, that is good because when it gets dark enough, you can see the stars. When it gets dark, even a little light will do. It is getting very dark—and that is especially true in condemnation, rejection, and dismissal of those who do not measure up.

There is a prominent American city where there is actually a sign posted that declares itself a city that "doesn't allow hate." That's nonsense. What the citizens and leadership mean—but will not say—is that it is a city where you are only allowed to hate the wrong people, hate the wrong political positions, and hate those whose positions contradict their politically correct positions. There are churches like that too. What if the first thing unbelievers thought of when they heard the word "church" or "Christian" was forgiveness?

Fairly recently a friend of mine—a fairly prominent Christian leader—did some really horrible and sinful things. As the Christian and secular social media, news media and publications attacked him, I was asked to make a comment on his actions. I refused. Actually, I was a bit stronger than that. I told my assistant to tell these inquirers where to go. She did not do that, but managed to convey my anger in her rejection of their requests.

Then, those same people attacking my friend turned their guns on me. Frankly, I did not care. One of the few good things about being old is that one really does not care. But that is not the important thing. What is important are the number of people who privately came to me afterward, discovering that I refused to join in with those who were throwing rocks. They wanted, believe it or not, to hear about Jesus.

When someone sins even big sins, there are two things that no one but God and that person knows. First, nobody knows the power of the temptation arrayed against that person. Sin is quite attractive. It never delivers on its promises, and its bite causes horrible wounds. But the mask it wears is pretty, and the siren call beckons with rapture, joy, and freedom. Believers sometimes forget.

Second, we have no idea how hard the person who sinned tried not to sin. I have often talked to people (those who trusted me with the truth) who have said to me, "Oh, Steve, you have no idea how hard I struggled." I did not.

When someone sins, quite often the first thing believers say is, "How could you?" Or, "After all that Jesus has done for you, your betrayal of him is unconscionable." That is among Christians, but it is also the same in the "gotcha" secular culture. If I had a dime for every time the social media and television pundits used the words "outraged," "infuriated," "offended," "insulted," and "incensed," I would be very rich.

A biblical response would be to cry with those who are weeping over their sin until the shame and shock get better. Utter the words of forgiveness. "It must have been horrible to cause you to go there" are healing words. Christians need to, as Luther said, preach the gospel to each other so they will not get discouraged. But we believers also need to preach the gospel to the marginalized, the fallen, the failures, the shamed, and the embarrassed of the world.

Christians need to offer the good news of God's forgiveness and acceptance to each other. But forgiveness is also what they are called to offer to the world. Grace levels the playing field, and it is a gift. It is actually fairly easy for a bad sinner to offer to cut slack to other bad sinners. When believers do not, Jesus leaves the building—and so do unbelievers.

Shock and Awe When Christians Show Up Unexpectedly

There is another place where Christians create shock and awe—when we show up in places where we are not expected. The Christian faith in the past has often been defined by what believers do not do, where they do not go, and what they refuse to countenance. That is, of course, sometimes a part of their witness. It wouldn't be seemly for a Christian to own a brothel, disown our children, or drink pagans under the table. But when we're defined by not wearing makeup, abstaining from dancing, staying away from movies, and refusing to associate with certain people, we may have separated ourselves from the real world so far that we no longer have a witness to that world.

I can remember the late Aiken Taylor (the editor of *Presbyterian Journal*, which later became *World* magazine) laughing about how Reformed Christians judged Reformed Christians from countries other than their own. The Germans were shocked that the Americans smoked, and the Americans were shocked that the Germans drank beer. Believers have often let the Christian subculture define what is appropriate and what is not when only God can do that. In 1 Corinthians 5:9–10, Paul corrects a misunderstanding of some Christians that they were to not associate with sinful unbelievers—because then, he said, Christians would "need to go out of the world" (v. 10).

I once lived in a development in Miami near a small hardware store. While the hardware store owner was reasonably civil when I shopped there, he was not friendly. In fact, I got the feeling that he wanted me to take my business somewhere else. I was not sure why he was so hostile but suspected that someone had told him that I was religious and maybe a pastor. That suspicion was confirmed when everything changed.

I love country music. Anna and I attended a Randy Travis concert (when his concerts were quite pagan and before he turned to mostly Christian music), and the arena where the concert was held was packed. It was great. But I did not think anybody would know I was there. I was wrong. Someone saw me there—the owner of that hardware store. Two days later when I entered his store, instead of wincing that the preacher had come again, the man welcomed me as his best friend.

"That Travis concert rocked!" he said. Then rather sheepishly he said, "I was kind of surprised to see you there." I am not saying that he fell on his knees and received Christ (it does not work that way), but I do know that if we had stayed in the area (we moved shortly after this incident), there would have been questions. He would not ask them in the store but maybe at dinner or over a beer. My new friend's questions would have been fairly subtle, but however he put them, he would have been curious about why someone who was religious would show at a concert that was not religious.

There are, of course, other items we could put on the list of how Christians create shock, awe, and questions—cutting slack in the hard places, refusing to be politically or religiously correct, never universalizing and applying personal proclivities in judging others, or maybe just doing something deemed inappropriate. As I said, you can make your own list.

After you do, go out and shock and awe someone, okay?

CHAPTER 10

Nobody's Mother

But [Jesus] said to him, "Man, who made me a judge
or arbitrator over you?" (Luke 12:14)

Tertullian—an early Christian theologian and often called
the father of western theology—addressed Rome: "We are but
of yesterday, and yet we have filled all the places that belong
to you—cities, islands, forts, towns, exchanges, the military
camps themselves, tribes, town councils, the palace, the senate,
the market-place; we have left you nothing but your temples."[1]
That is still true. Christians are sort of like weeds. They are
everywhere.

In the places where they live and work, Christians' concern and compassion is generally the natural demeanor. When
one encounters Christians who do not care, it is aberrant and
abnormal, and something is wrong. However, as good as that
is, there is an attached problem.

Religion in general, and Christianity in particular, can
make people weird. One of the major ways it will do that is to
give them a sense of responsibility for everything that happens

in the world. The process starts with caring, compassion, and concern. Then, if converts are not careful, it can morph into something that is not Christian at all: a neurotic mother complex. I have a pastor friend who told me once that he found it hard to find a "balance between not giving a damn and caring too much." I suspect that most Christians struggle with the same balance.

Thomas Kelly (the American Quaker, educator, and mystic), in his book *A Testament of Devotion,* writes with great insight about a believer's limitations and the necessity of particularization (i.e., thinking that everything bad is a call for every Christian to get involved):

> But it is a particularization of my responsibility in a world too vast and a lifetime too short for me to carry all responsibilities. My cosmic love, or the Divine Lover loving within me, cannot accomplish its full intent, which is universal saviorhood, within the limits of three score years and ten. But the Loving Presence does not burden us equally with all things, but considerately puts upon each of us just a few central tasks, as emphatic responsibilities. For each of us these special undertakings are our share in the joyous burdens of love.
>
> Thus the state of having a concern has a foreground and a background. In the foreground is the special task, uniquely illuminated toward which we feel a special yearning and care. But in the background is a second level, or layer, of universal concern for all the multitude of good things that need doing. Toward them all we feel kindly, but we are dismissed from active service in most of them. And we have an easy mind in the presence of desperately real needs which are not our direct responsibility. We cannot die on every cross, nor are we expected to.[2]

My former student Dwight Bain is now a Christian counselor, with a large practice in Orlando. We were talking recently about how Christians often assume responsibility for what is not theirs. Dwight was laughing about the time he came to me with some major concerns for the African nation of Zimbabwe, and he remembered me asking him if he could spell Zimbabwe. He could not. I then asked him if he had ever been to Zimbabwe, and he had not. "Then it's not yours," I told him.

Christians really cannot hang on every cross, die on every hill, and fix every problem. Christians must be sensitive to the Holy Spirit's acts of particularization. I once expressed my feelings of guilt to my friend Eddie Waxer, who runs a sports ministry. I was feeling guilty about not being more involved in his sports ministry and in another friend Cleve Bell's (Riverside House) prison ministry. "Are you crazy?" Eddie said to me. "You know nothing about sports and if you got involved with me or with Cleve's prison work, you would make a fool of yourself and would make a mess of it. For our sakes, stick to where God has called you, not where God has called *us*." Good point.

The neurotic-mother complex can become quite destructive of believers' effort to communicate the truth of the Christian faith to those who do not want to hear it. Christian compassion and concern often degenerates into moralism, manipulation, and abuse of power. When that happens, we believers feel good about ourselves because we—even if nobody else thinks so—are doing it for their good and out of love. Actually, most of the time we are not. My late mentor Fred Smith used to say that Christians know that unbelievers are in for an unpleasant surprise when they enter eternity, but we want to rob them of any enjoyment before they get there.

Am I saying that Christians do not have a responsibility for others? Of course not. It is important that they speak truth to power, vote, and take public stands on social issues addressed in Scripture. Abortion, sex trafficking, racism, hunger, abuse, justice, and a host of other issues are all a proper concern for Christians. God has, by his grace, given clear direction for culture and life. However, sometimes Christians go much further than his clear direction. We believers decide that it is our responsibility to correct every sin, straighten out every silly and spurious comment, and fix every injustice. First, we cannot do all of that. And second, we are not called to do all of that. We have been trying to play mother to people who simply do not want or need a mother.

Playing off the first of the old four spiritual laws, "God loves you and has a wonderful plan for your life," my colleague Erik Guzman would often say, "God loves me, and Steve has a wonderful plan for my life." If you have an agenda for someone else, stop it. There are few things more irritating and more of a hindrance to real communication than trying to be someone's mother.

Christian accountability groups can gather together to run each other's lives. Prayer circles are often where prayers become sermons. Personal proclivities become universals that are applied to brothers and sisters. Christians mother each other with subtle hints and outright criticisms, when they simply have not earned the right to be heard.

Jinx is a gifted staff member who produces some of Key Life's programs and works with the technical side of the ministry. He also has long hair that makes him look like Jesus. When we met, the first thing I said to him was, "Son, get a haircut!" It took him a good while to realize that I was joking. If you have ever seen me, you know that I am bald. Now when I tell Jinx that he should get a haircut, he responds, "I'll get a haircut when you grow hair." But even now, after we have been friends for a good many years, Jinx still winces when I tell him to get a haircut. Do you know why? Too many mothers said that to him, and they were not joking.

Paul was talking about believers when he wrote, "As for the one who is weak in faith, welcome him, but not to quarrel over opinions. . . . Who are you to pass judgment on the servant of another? It is before his own master that he stands or falls" (Romans 14:1, 4). Paul could have said the same thing about our relationship to unbelievers. And even if he did not, I am.

Mothers in the Small Stuff

People who do not know the truth may think that a lot of what Christians believe is small, insignificant stuff. It is important that Christians stop majoring in what unbelievers think are minors. That was Paul's attitude when he wrote to the Philippians that he was quite aware that some preachers were con artists preaching Christ out of selfishness. Nonetheless, Paul wrote, "What then? Only that in every way, whether in pretense or in truth, Christ is proclaimed, and in that I rejoice" (Philippians 1:18).

Jesus had the same attitude. One time, John told Jesus that he had encountered some people who were using the name of Christ and that he forbade them because they were not "following us." Jesus replied, "Do not stop him, for no one who does a mighty work in my name will be able soon afterward to speak evil of me. For the one who is not against us is for us" (Mark 9:38–40).

Everything is small stuff except Jesus, especially when Christians are trying to communicate truth to unbelievers. That small stuff is way above the Christian's pay grade, and when believers spend time on it, they sound like very angry and uptight mothers. The condemnation, correction, and admonishments are not helpful. The message should be, "Jesus loves you, and I'm trying. I don't care what your sexual proclivity is, whom you voted for, who you hate and who you love, or where you hang out, and Jesus doesn't either. Run to him and you might be surprised." If unbelievers heard that message (as antinomian as it sounds), the gospel would once again be attractive to the world.

Scott Ross had been a New York DJ connected to the Rolling Stones and Bob Dylan, and he acted as master of ceremonies for one of the Beatles' concerts at Shea Stadium. I heard him speak shortly after he became a Christian. While his newfound faith left a lot to be desired, he was right on when he said that he was thankful that Christians did not talk to him about his drugs but about Jesus. In other words, he said those Christians refused to be his mother. If they had tried to play that role, Scott might have died from the drugs instead of being made alive by Christ.

Mothers Who Are Social Critics

Another way Christians become mothers is when they try to become social critics for what is wrong with the world. Of course, Christians need to speak truth about social issues. The problem happens when their stand for social issues becomes the definition of who they are. It is like the painting instructor who told his student who was paining a barn, "Son, there's a sunset behind the barn. You don't have time to paint the barn and the sunset. You have to choose." Christians do not have time to be both inappropriate mothers and to love at the same time, and so it is important that we choose.

Dr. Ken Blanchard, in his successful leadership book *The One Minute Manager*,[3] makes a pretty radical and effective point, and writes about it further on his website. "I believe," Blanchard writes, "the key to developing employees and building a great organization is to wander around and catch people doing things right. This is a powerful management concept that isn't used as often as it should be. Unfortunately, most leaders tend to focus on the things that are being done wrong so they can fix them."[4]

Christians can take that very wise advice and apply it to their witness to the world. My mother always knew when I was doing something wrong, and was never reticent about addressing it. My father, on the other hand, knew too but did not talk about it much. I suppose that both reactions to my doing something wrong were needful. But Christians should be more like my father and less like my mother in their relationship with unbelievers.

One of core principles we teach at Key Life is that radical grace does not work unless one knows that one is a radical sinner—as in, "You wouldn't be so shocked at your own sin if you didn't have such a high opinion of yourself." In the context of radical and pervasive sinfulness (clearly taught in the Bible), faithfulness, mercy, and compassion (even if skewed) are to be encouraged and praised. The grace of God, which is radically necessary for all people, really does level the playing field.

I have watched my neighbors (often unbelievers) help one another after the devastation of a hurricane. I have seen overworked, secular organizations provide help to those who were helpless. I have watched my political adversaries show compassion. I have watched pro-choice women care about scared and pregnant girls, a strip-club owner who welcomed Christians to his club because they were a positive influence on his strippers, lesbian and gay friends weep over the pain and loss of others after a shooting at a gay bar, and all kinds of surprising small acts of kindness coming from very unexpected and secular quarters. Does that change my negative view of human nature? Of course not. But what would happen if I pointed *those* things out, rather than throw my rocks?

This is something I struggle with, and always have. I have very strong political, social, philosophical, and cultural views—and frankly, I think they are right, true, and proper. Others just say that I am insufferably opinionated. I am also a teacher, and teachers have a proclivity to straighten out things they think are not true. I am learning to keep my opinions to myself in a lot of areas where I do not need to say anything, and to be far more gentle and kind in areas where I am constrained to speak. I am old, and a part of that restraint is age. But I trust some of it is Jesus. Paul wrote to his young friend Timothy about the importance of being faithful even sharing the sufferings of Christ. Then he adds, "No soldier gets entangled in civilian pursuits, since his aim is to please the one who enlisted him" (2 Timothy 2:4).

Years ago my friend Randy Pope, the pastor of Perimeter Church in Atlanta, was one of the first Presbyterians to use contemporary worship forms. He even took off his tie when he preached. Presbyterians always do things decently and in order. Contemporary music and informal dress are not decent and, in fact, to many Presbyterians they are unseemly. Randy received a lot of criticism (and still does). Once when he addressed the general assembly of our denomination, he said to his critics, "Would you take off your tie if you knew that taking it off would bring one person to Christ? How about bringing a drum to a worship service if you knew that people would see Jesus?" Randy was simply saying that some things are more important than others, and that the most important of all is Jesus.

Christians are not called to straighten out the world of unbelievers. We are not their mothers. But what about looking for what is good, and affirming it, in unbelievers? What would happen if Christians were less critical and more affirming? Would you be willing to rein in your political and even moral views if you knew that people would come to Christ because you did?

Mothers Who Preach without Illustrating

Let me give you another way Christians develop a mother complex: they do it by elucidating rather than illustrating. In other words, believers think that their preaching is more effective than a silent illustration of the truths they believe. It is said that St. Francis said that Christians should preach the gospel and, when absolutely necessary, use words (he probably did not, but it is still a good thought). There is an old story of the time that St. Francis and his simple friars came to a village and discovered that the village church had changed its name to "The Church of St. Francis." He directed his followers to tear down that church rock by rock. As they left the village, one of the friars said to St. Francis that he thought they had come to the village to preach the gospel. St. Francis replied simply, "We did."

I agree with the view that Christians are the measurement of what the world sees about the Christian faith. The trouble is that being a proper and adequate measure is often conflated with being pure, obedient, faithful, and nice. The implication is that if Christians are not these things, they will hurt their witness. No, actually that is not what hurts their witness. I rarely come across someone who became a Christian because of another Christian's goodness. That is not even our witness.

My wife and I spent the last three months of my mother's life living with her in the mountains of North Carolina. We always had a place for her in our home in Florida, and expected that the time would come when she would no longer be able to take care of herself and that she would come to live with us. God had other plans. He allowed our home—along with the place in our home we had prepared for her—to be destroyed by Hurricane Andrew. When my mother's doctor called me and said she was terminal and that something needed to be done, my wife and I decided to move to North Carolina and live with her for the duration. During that time, I did Key Life broadcasts from the back porch of the home where I grew up and handled the business of the ministry with my phone and computer. In between, my wife and I helped my mother die. Well, maybe "helped her die" is not the best description; she needed very little help.

Her friends came in droves to say goodbye to her, and neighbors would check in on her to see if there was anything she needed. She gave instructions on marriage (and everything else) to her grandsons and granddaughters. She expressed her fear and her faith with such authenticity that everybody who knew her was amazed. She continued to read the Bible and Spurgeon, to pray, and for as long as she could, attend church. And she got every relationship fixed, apologized for things she had said, was sometimes inappropriate, and seemed even less than Christian when she laughed at the jokes she found funny. As I watched my mother die—and I was holding her hand when she did—I wanted to take out an ad in the local newspaper to invite others to "come and see a godly woman die!"

That is the mantra of Christians who have decided not to be the mother of the world: "Come and watch!" See the human side of the faith—the failure and the success, the laughter and the tears, the love and the not so loving, and the reality of those who know that life is about Jesus and that he is enough.

For some reason, when I was a pastor, I started saying from the pulpit, "I'm not your mother." To be honest, I started saying it because it had a nice postmodern ring to it. Eventually, it became a regular occurrence with a more focused purpose. I remember saying once, "If you don't buy into this Christian thing, that's okay. However, you ought to get some benefit from attending church and I'm here to help. Read the Bible. You say, 'I don't believe the Bible.' That's okay, I'm not your mother. 'But I don't even believe in God.' Again, I'm not your mother. But listen to me: if you read the Bible and try to conform your life to it as much as you can, even if you don't believe it, you will sleep better at night, you'll feel better about the world, you'll be a much nicer person, and people will like you more. As I said, I'm not your mother and you can do what you want. But if you try it and it helps, you don't have to thank me. I was glad to help."

Do you know what I discovered? I found unbelievers drawn to what I was saying, and many of them even became Christians. I discovered that they were drawn to the warmth of our fire, and that the last thing they wanted was a mother. They already had one of those.

Nobody needs more than one.

CHAPTER 11

Roaring Lambs

In God . . . I trust; I shall not be afraid. What can flesh do to me? (Psalm 56:4)

The title of this chapter comes from a book written by my late friend Bob Briner, titled *Roaring Lambs: A Gentle Plan to Radically Change Your World.*[1] The main thesis of that book is that roaring lambs (that would be believers) ought to infiltrate and make an impact on the world. Someone has said that Bob was talking about putting shoe leather to one's faith. That is the main thesis of this chapter, too.

There is a serious problem with that, though. Most Christians (me included, sometimes) are so unsure in our faith and worried about what others will say, we think that if we try to go out into an unbelieving world with our faith, it will be destroyed. Our faith is not much, but it is all we have. We have decided to protect it at all costs. The only place we feel safe with our faith is in church, and even there it is iffy.

I am going to teach you how to cuss. I know, I am ordained, and that is not what preachers generally do. Repeat after me: *Quid inferorum!* That is Latin for "What the hell?" If you learn to use it, people will think you are smart, and uptight Christians won't know you are cursing.

Quid inferorum is the attitude that ought to be a significant part of a Christian's witness and walk. In fact, I would suggest that only Christians can adopt that attitude because we are the only ones who are (or should be) free enough to live that way.

I want to remind believers of some things that they already knew; but as with Luther's comment that Christians should preach the gospel to each other lest they become discouraged, I am going to preach these facts to myself and to you, lest we both become afraid and hide. The truth is that Christians ought to be dangerous—and we are not.

Jonathan Merritt, in his very good book *Learning to Speak God from Scratch: Why Sacred Words Are Vanishing—and How We Can Revive Them,* talks about moving from the Bible belt of Atlanta to New York City where, to his surprise, he ran into a "language barrier":

> To avoid having to define every sacred term, I swept them into a pile and out the door. Not wanting to be associated with those in society who spoke God fluently but irresponsibly, I started avoiding spiritual conversations altogether.
>
> I am not alone. I've been meeting people from all over, with similar histories of belief, who feel they too have been struck mute in a strange land. Terms like sin and hell have become so negative they lodge in our throats. Others, like *belief* and *salvation* have been uttered so often we don't know what they mean anymore. Definitions and connotations of words like *mercy* and *love* can no longer be assumed.[2]

A Christian should be dangerous—a "roaring lion." The problem is that they have been silenced—or, as it were, defanged.

The defanging has happened, at least partially, because believers have forgotten some basic facts about themselves that need to be affirmed and underlined often. We Christians need to review some of these facts with the purpose of motivating ourselves to go anywhere, be with anybody, speak any truth, show up at any event, laugh at any joke, weep at any tragedy, accept any aberration, and worship at no altar but the altar of Jesus. We will be dangerous when love and freedom define us. And because of that definition, we will find that we are answering long-silenced questions that are again asked by unbelievers.

The Sovereignty of God

The first fact—and perhaps the most important—is that God really is in charge, and he knows what he is doing. Ron Dunn, the late international Bible teacher, used to say that God not only knows what he's doing, he does it right well. Jude's benediction is right on, "Now to him who is able to keep you from stumbling and to present you blameless before the presence of his glory with great joy, to the only God, our Savior, through Jesus Christ our Lord, be glory, majesty, dominion, and authority, before all time and now and forever" (Jude 24–25).

Many believers are like the preacher who was playing golf when a squirrel took his lost ball, ran to the green, and dropped it in the hole. The preacher looked up to the sky and said, "Please Father, I would rather do it myself!" It is quite irritating to think that we might not be, as William Henley said in his poem "Invictus," the masters of our fates and the captains of our souls. Our desire to do it ourselves has tremendous theological implications, and among them is the promotion of our self-righteous efforts at obedience in cheapening God's demands at the expense of God's holiness.

There are also social implications with the motivational nonsense, promoting the lie that Christians can "just do it," and thus achieve every dream they ever had. Our desire to do it ourselves gives credence to the belief that the unfixable can be fixed, and every problem has a solution. When Jesus said, "For you always have the poor with you" (Matthew 26:11), he was not suggesting that believers just ignore the poor; he was simply looking at a world where effort and resolution do not always go together.

I once attended a very large Christian conference during the early days of the debates about gay marriage. Banners all over the large hotel said that "Western Civilization" was in the balance, and that if we as a culture affirmed gay marriage, Western culture would go down in flames. One of the banners read, "If you're not part of the solution, you're the problem." Everywhere I looked, signs urged that I "take a stand." Even then (and I had not, up to that point, thought much about the issue), it seemed to me that was insane. Western civilization may be in the balance for a lot of reasons, and it is not because of same-sex marriage. I affirm traditional marriage and think that it is an important issue, but frankly, I do not lose sleep over who people marry.

God's sovereignty relieves me of a great responsibility—the responsibility of assuming the role of God. No matter what I do, say, or think, no matter if I succeed or fail, no matter if I do it right or wrong, God is still in charge, things are under his control, and in the end, "every knee should bow, in heaven and on earth and under the earth" (Philippians 2:10).

As I write this, there is an election coming up. I have already mentioned my conservative political convictions. This morning, I prayed a panic prayer, telling God what ought to happen. I had been watching way too many news programs and listening to way too many experts who did not know any more than I did. I had honestly come to the belief that the world as we know it would come to an end if certain politicians (those, of course, who agree with me) were not elected. As I prayed, I sensed that God asked, "Are you going to vote?" I told him that of course I was going to vote.

"Then what else are you going to do?"

I thought about it—and realized that there was nothing else I *could* do. I think God said, "Then why not let me do the rest? You can go to sleep and I'll stay up."

Repeat after me: *Quid inferorum!* There now, do you feel better?

Christians Do Not Have Anything to Protect or Lose

Another truth that flows from God's sovereignty is that Christians do not have anything to protect or lose. When Paul said in Romans that we should consider/reckon ourselves dead (Romans 6:11), it sounds like bad news. Actually, it is good news and points to what should and should not be important to dead people: not much. Paul said, "if we live, we live to the Lord, and if we die, we die to the Lord. So then [*Quid inferorum*], whether we live or whether we die, we are the Lord's" (Romans 14:8—I appropriately added the Latin).

Life is not an effort to get the most toys (or degrees, dates, or data) and win the game. Seeing oneself as dead but alive in Christ changes everything. Christians who are dead but alive in Christ do not need to spend undue time protecting what they have and acquiring more. I once heard that C. S. Lewis said that the only books believers would have in heaven would be books they loaned out, gave away, or which were stolen. I do not know for sure if that is true, but I now look at books differently than I used to. I have a fairly extensive library; when people borrowed books from me, I required that they sign a form and told them that if the book was not returned, they would get the hives. When people pilfered books from me, I would pray that they die a horrible death. Not really, but I did spend a great deal of time protecting my library. Not anymore. I rarely read a book twice, I have the entire Internet to do research, and I do not have any more space on my bookshelves. But more than that, I just do not care.

When we went through Hurricane Andrew a number of years ago, my wife and I lost almost all our stuff along with

111

our house. Shortly after that, our contractor went bankrupt and, when he went down, he took a good deal of the insurance money with him. We were forced to live in a very small apartment (the size of a dorm room) with one window looking out on a brick wall. It was not a pleasant time. One morning, I went out to the parking lot to discover that someone had stolen my car. The car was not in great shape (a tree had fallen on it during the hurricane), but it was the only car I had. If someone had stolen it the previous year, I would have first told Jesus that he did not love me, and that if he did I would still have my car. Then I would have gotten my gun and gone looking for the culprit.

But do you know what I did? Even now it is hard to believe that I was that wise—I started laughing. I went back to our small apartment and told my wife that someone had stolen "God's car." She started laughing, too. In fact, we got the giggles and found it hard to stop. It really did not matter. Dead people are not overly concerned with cars.

I have a pastor friend around my age who told me that he had decided to only spend time with people who would cry at his funeral. "At my age," he said, "my time is limited and those who wouldn't give a rip about my death are not the people I want to be with." I have been thinking about that, and he is right. It cuts back on social obligations, reminds me to number my days, and reminds me who and what is important.

Today's culture does its best to mask the grim reality of death. The funeral business tries to make the corpse look alive and cover the casket with flowers. I often read news articles that report on the scientific findings regarding a particular food or medication. Those articles claim, "The death rate is 20 percent higher for. . . ." What? The death rate is the same, and that statistic never changes. It is one out of one. No matter what people eat or drink, what medications they take, or how much they exercise, in the end they are going to die. I am not altogether happy with that. Nobody is. But hiding that reality hinders people from determining what is important while they are still alive. There is an incredible freedom in knowing what is important and what is not. That freedom makes Christians dangerous, roaring lions.

There was a missionary who was told on the trip to a violent country that he would die if he continued his journey there. He laughed and said, "I died before I got on this boat." Dead people who are still alive are free and dangerous, because they do not care about what everybody says. In fact, they can laugh and say, *Quid inferorum!*

Try it, and see if you do not feel better.

Christians Do Not Have to Be Right

Another area of great freedom for Christians is that they do not have to be right anymore. Paul, at one time, was quite in-your-face with his adversary in an ecclesiastical meeting. In fact, Paul called one of them a "whitewashed wall." That is so very human, but that is not what was important. The important thing was Paul's quick apology. Paul says, "I did not know, brothers, that he was the high priest, for it is written, 'You shall not speak evil of a ruler of your people'" (Acts 23:3, 5). When I read that passage, I want to say to Paul, "Stick to your guns! He probably is a whitewashed wall and once you say it, don't back off." But Paul did not do that. He did not have to be right.

Vested interest happens whenever people make a public commitment to a person, program, or party. That is, of course, doubly true when believers are talking about the church or Christianity. After all, when God gets involved, and people are on God's side, their position must be defended at all costs.

No, it does not. In fact, when people are talking about God, it stands to reason that much of their talk will be in error. His thoughts are not human thoughts and his ways not human ways (Isaiah 55:8). If that is true (and it is), then we are all going to get it wrong, and some of us are going to get it really wrong.

It drives me nuts when in response to the question of what denomination someone is in or what church one attends, someone says, "I'm only a Christian." I want to say, "Yeah, and one with no convictions!" I am not suggesting that Christians go out into the world with no convictions, but I am suggesting that believers do not have to share everything they know with everybody they meet. I am also suggesting that most battles over who is right or who is wrong rarely convince those with a different position. More importantly, the list of convictions held by Christians should be far shorter than it is. The world is big enough for all Christians to be wrong a lot, and some convictions are so esoteric that nobody cares.

When I was in graduate school, I was taught the Graf-Wellhausen hypothesis (or documentary hypothesis). I have serious problems with that whole thing, I think it is outdated, and I believe that it comes more from unbelief than scholarship. Do you know how many people care what I think about that hypothesis? I cannot think of any. In fact, opinions on the issue cannot be surveyed because people will not have the foggiest idea what the questions even mean. It's the same with my political, sociological, and even some of my theological views—all of which I believe are correct and proper.

Who cares? Nobody.

Most Christians see postmodernity (or whatever one calls the cultural shift through which the world has gone) as a very negative thing. There is something to that assessment. However, in many ways, today's culture has some positives. For instance, for the first time in my memory Christians have a level playing field in their conversations with unbelievers. Nothing has to be proven and, if Christians do not blow it, they can get a hearing.

I used to teach a seminary course titled "Communicating to Postmoderns." In that course, I challenged students to head to downtown Orlando and strike up a conversation with the most out-of-the-box people they could find. I told them, "If you listen as much as you talk, if you don't bring your agenda, if you take off your tie, and if you don't pretend to have all the answers, you will be heard." It was surprising how many of those students discovered that what I taught them was true.

One of the great hindrances to the Christian effort to share our faith is the horrible need to correct every error. When unbelievers say things like, "I used to be a part of the church but there was so much hypocrisy in it that I couldn't remain any longer," do you know what my first reaction is? It is to say that they are shallow, sophomoric, and silly. The fact is, that may exactly be what that kind of comment reflects; and if you wanted me to do it, I would be glad to give you a list of reasons why it is shallow, sophomoric, and silly. And that is why I have trouble getting unbelievers to listen to me. I get reminded often that I do not have to protect or defend the church, my Christian faith, or my commitments. I really do not, and you do not have to either.

The church has been around a long time and has buried most of its critics. It still does. Not only that, there is hardly anything negative that one can say about the church that is not at least partially true, and there is hardly anything positive that one can say about the church that is not at least partially true. Christians are a bad bunch (the Bible is clear on that), and when someone points that out, a proper response should be "duh!"

Or maybe, *Quid inferorum.* You will feel better if you do say this. You might also even feel free to say something about Jesus.

Christians Do Not Have to Pretend

Another truth that can make a difference is that Christians do not have to pretend to be good and together, or bad and messed up. Paul said that he was the "chief of sinners," and in Romans 7, he even confesses his sins in a very public way. If you want to read Paul's rather long list of the good stuff he did, read 2 Corinthians 11.

A number of years ago, I was interviewed to do a syndicated weekly television show. The director, who was not a believer, looked me up and down and said, "Steve, you're ugly." Then she smiled, "Ugly . . . but your face has character." I got the job, and I have lived on the "face with character" comment for a long time. When I look in the mirror I think, *I'm ugly, but it's okay because I have a face with great character.* In other words, there is the good and the bad. In fact, that is true of my life. There are areas where I am faithful and could even be called good, and then there are other areas much less so. Now with the freedom that acceptance gives me—acceptance from the only one who matters, God—I have the freedom to take off my mask and to live my life in the joy of no longer having to wear it.

And no, that does not contradict other things I have said about human depravity. There is always sin. Smiling and pretending that Christians are without sin or pain creates heels and elbows as unbelievers run in the other direction. Pretending that we believers are ugly and that our mother dresses us funny (that's false humility, because God doesn't make junk) does exactly the same thing. At the very base of our nature is our great need for a great Savior, because we really are great sinners. But there are some attractive qualities in Christians that God gave them even before they met Jesus.

I recently preached in a large church with three services. Because Key Life often videos places where I speak, my assistant was asked which of the three services Key Life wanted to use. She asked me, and I said, "The second one. By the time I got to the third one I was too full of myself. And in the first service all I worried about was what people would think." My assistant told the church that we would like a video of the second service. When she was asked why, my assistant told them what I said. They just laughed and said that they had not noticed. A few years ago, I would have been mortified if my assistant had said that to strangers. Now (that is, now that I am quite spiritual), it does not bother me at all. I have learned that preachers who are never ego-driven, never full of themselves instead of Christ, and who are always focused on God's people instead of what God's people are thinking about them are either lying or very poor preachers. When that happens, repentance is in order, then climbing back in the pulpit as soon as possible and doing better.

By "doing better," I do not mean working hard to be pure. That is not going to happen. And I also do not mean telling people that one is really bad and they just have to deal with it, thereby creating authenticity. Rather, it means being more concerned with Jesus than one's perfection or lack thereof.

By the way, believers who are not preachers deal with exactly the same issue. Change the circumstance, substitute your name or the word "Christian" for "preacher," and the Holy Spirit will convict you too. Trust me on this.

I once interviewed Jim Bakker on a television program. Jim Bakker was a famous and popular televangelist, and along with his wife Tammy Faye founded a large religious television empire. Then there was the fall. He was accused of sexual sins, misusing ministry money, and fraud. Bakker went through a divorce, his empire crumbled, and he went to prison. My interview with him took place shortly after he had been released from prison. I wish I had the space to describe that interview. There were tears (real tears), laughter (free and without rancor), and an incredible reality about him that I had not noticed in all of his years on television.

I asked Bakker what was different now that he had walked through so much humiliation and rejection. He thought for a moment and said, "The difference is that now I can go anywhere and talk to anybody about anything, and they will listen." He paid a big price for that credibility. Drunks will not listen to anybody but drunks. Addicts will not listen to anybody but addicts. Sinners will not listen to anybody but sinners. Normal people who know they are bad with some good parts will not listen to anybody except those who are bad with some good parts. If you have a message for alcoholics, you had better know what it was like to make a fool of yourself when you were drunk. If you are thinking about a ministry to addicts, you had better be able to know the midnight cravings when the demons come, and you thought you were going to die. And if you have a passion to reach sinners, you had better be able to say, "Been there and done that, and sometimes still go there and do that." If you want to reach your neighbor, be human and free. In other words, just be who you are. Then they will listen.

The next time someone finds out that you are not as good, pure, or faithful as they thought you were, or as bad as you could be, do not try and correct the perceptions. Do not defend or explain. Say "bingo," and then tell them what is really important.

Or alternatively, say *Quid inferorum*. You will feel better, and they will listen.

Christians Do Not Have Anything to Hide

Another fact about Christians is that they really do not have anything to hide.

The late Bruce Thielemann was a friend of mine, and one of the finest Christian communicators I have ever heard. He was the pastor of Glendale Presbyterian Church in California and First Presbyterian Church in Pittsburgh; toward the end of his life, he was the dean of the chapel at Grove City College. Bruce was a lifelong bachelor and as such sometimes struggled with loneliness. One time, when Bruce was living in California and came back from a fairly extended mission trip to Africa, as he looked out over Glendale from his apartment window, he was hit hard with an almost unbearable loneliness. Bruce got on the phone and started calling pastor friends in Glendale to see if he could meet with them. In each case, the pastor friend replied that it would be fine and said, "let me get my calendar." They found a time for lunch a week or more into the future.

When Bruce called the last pastor on his list, the pastor said, "Let me check my calendar."

"No," Bruce said, "I'm not going to wait. I need a brother right now." His friend tried to get out of it but finally said that he would meet Bruce that day for lunch.

When they met, Bruce poured out his heart and the pain of his loneliness. His friend said, "Do you know why I tried to stonewall you about this lunch?" Bruce allowed that he did not, and his friend said, "Last night I went home and found my wife in the arms of another man." If they were paying attention, people in that restaurant would have noticed two pastors holding hands and crying together. Bruce said that Christians are to "Bear one another's burdens" (Galatians 6:2), but that it was impossible to bear one another's burdens without first sharing those burdens.

It always amazes me how Christians follow a Messiah who ended up on a cross and told them that they had to carry one too, yet still talk about the victorious Christian life. Victorious living is sometimes barely keeping your nose above water, sinning a little less on occasion than you did before, and getting up in the morning to face the pain of a bad marriage, a cancer prognosis, or a rebellious child when you would rather just stay in bed. When Christians pretend that is not true, nobody wants to listen when they talk about Christ. If believers are not clear that the Christian faith is not pain without pressure but pain *under* pressure, those who face their own pressure will not give a rip about the message.

Years ago I had a friend, Blair Richardson, who died when he was young. Blair was an incredible Christian and a prizefighter (he held the middleweight title in Canada). He would often go into the slums of Boston, set up a fighting ring in a public place, and teach young people about prizefighting— always with a good word about Jesus and how Jesus had changed Blair's life. At the time of his death, Blair was a professor of communications at a major university in Boston and married to his wife Beverly, who was pregnant with their first child. Then Blair died, following surgery for a brain tumor. I still think of Blair and remember the weekend after his death when he was scheduled to speak to the young people at the church where I was pastor. I remember telling those young people why Blair would not be coming to our event.

When my friend John DeBrine, who was Blair and Beverly's pastor, met with Beverly after Blair's death, he said to her, "Beverly, this is so hard and I know it. I loved Blair, too. People have always looked at you with envy. You are beautiful, you were married to a guy who looked like a Greek god, you are expecting your first child, and you had an idyllic life. They have always said about you when they heard your testimony, 'Sure, if I had her life I would be a Christian too.' Beverly, they are still listening. Don't hide your pain, use it."

When Christians hide their pain, they do not have a message to give. Life really is not for sissies, and the difference between a Christian and an unbeliever is Jesus. He is all. If believers can say *Quid inferorum* in the midst of their pain, others will listen to their message, and Christians will feel better saying it.

Christians Do Not Have Anything to Promote

There is one final fact. Christians do not have anything to promote. When Paul wrote to the church at Corinth he said, "I decided to know nothing among you except Jesus Christ and him crucified" (1 Corinthians 2:2). He did not just say that. Paul had a side job, so he did not even have to make his living from his faith.

Now that is refreshing.

Did you hear about the pastor who went to the train station every day in town and just stood there, watching the train go through? The church leaders went to their pastor and told him that they liked his sermons and his pastoral work, but that these visits were causing people to talk. They asked him why he did it. "It's simple," the pastor said. "I go there because it is refreshing to see something go through this town that I don't have to push." The problem with the message that Christians have for the world is that there is almost always something attached to it. It seems that believers are always pushing something.

Christians are always trying to get something from somebody (even good things), and that gets mixed in with the message they have been given. We believers want others to join our church, become a part of some program, sign a petition, or contribute to a cause, and those people never hear the message we have been called to speak. There is always an angle and, because there is, people are weary of our message. What if we just said, in effect, "I don't want anything from you. I just wanted you to know that Jesus loves you and doesn't want anything either. Is that okay?"

I have only been through one church building program in my long ministry. In fact, I think that you should not seek advice from any pastor who has been through more than one. One building program can be marked up to inexperience, but more than that reveals something seriously bent about that pastor (not really . . . but sort of). That building program was one of the worst experiences of my life. I will spare you the details, but I did everything wrong—the building committee resigned, and I have never had so many people angry at me at the same time. I complained to a pastor friend, who told me that once we laid our first brick all the problems would stop. So I appointed a building committee of two friends and said, "In two weeks we're having a groundbreaking ceremony out there in the parking lot. I don't care if we build an outhouse, but we're going to build something."

My friend turned out to be right. We finally completed the building project, and it was quite nice. People who had told me, "You can't do that," started saying, "Look what we did!"

During that building program, a church member wanted to give me his two-year-old Cadillac. That kind of thing never happened to me except this once. When I declined, he said, "Just come over and sit in it. You'll love it." I laughed and said, "Not a chance! Can you imagine me trying to raise all this money for the building program, and asking people to give sacrificially, while driving around in a Cadillac?" I said from the pulpit that I had some difficult things to teach and "as soon as I can raise the money for this building, you should get out of the way." Everybody laughed because they thought it was a joke.

The hardest thing about the building program was that I always had it hanging over my head. There was not a sermon I preached, a conversation I had, or a relationship that I valued that did not have that building program, and all the money that needed to be raised, mixed into it.

One Sunday morning, when the elders were meeting for prayer before service, a man came into my study. He had given five thousand dollars to the building program, and then became its chief critic. Almost every week, he complained about something, pushed his agendas, and criticized those who were working on the building program. When this man came into my study that morning, the elders were shocked at what I said to him, "Sam (not his name), I don't want to hear it! That's all that five thousand buys you. If you want to give more money, I'll listen to more of your nonsense. But no more. You've used up your gift."

Of course, he left the church, but I felt so free. It was the first time in a good while that I spoke truth without an agenda (although I repented of my harshness later). It was a good feeling. It was like saying *Quid inferorum*, and it felt good.

So much in this book is about attitude. It really is the key to communicating truth effectively to people who do not want to hear it, or who think they do not want to hear it. The bottom line is that a lot of our communication gets mixed up with so many other things—like the building program, in my case—and prevents the truth from being spoken clearly, lovingly, and without any expectation. If you thought I was really teaching you how to cuss in Latin here, you have not understood this chapter. I have been talking about an attitude that comes from walking with Jesus, who says that we should "go into all the world" and he would go with us—reminding us that we are loved, forgiven, acceptable, and free.

You cannot do that (or at least, I cannot) without remembering, thinking, and sometimes saying *Quid inferorum*. That is what makes Christians dangerous.

CHAPTER 12

Hey, Let's Be Careful Out There!

Behold, I am sending you out as sheep in the midst of wolves, so be wise as serpents and innocent as doves. (Matthew 10:16)

The only time (both the first and the last) I have gone snow skiing was in Switzerland, when my wife and I were staying with some friends. Our friends grew up on skis, and assumed that everybody was born knowing how to ski. They felt that a day on the major slopes would be fun for me.

It was not.

They put me on a major slope without a single skiing lesson. As I went down that slope at increasing speeds, I remembered that nobody told me how to stop. Well, I knew how to stop, but was not happy with the prospect that I could, moving at such a tremendous speed, run into a tree. It quickly became apparent to me that I was going to die.

The only reason I did not die was because one of my Swiss friends noticed my panic, skied down the slope beside me, held out his ski pole, and told me to hold onto it. With him holding the other end, we slowed down and eventually reached the bottom of the slope safely. When I thought I was going to die, I made a promise to God that, if he got me down from that mountain alive, I would never ski again. I have kept that promise.

I did, however, learn a principle that day: never take advice from anybody about anything that is hard—unless the one giving that advice knows just how hard it is.

I have been speaking truth to people who did not want to hear it for a very long time, and I know how hard that is. There have been times when I did it right, and a whole lot of times I did it wrong. Sometimes I have been winsome in doing it and sometimes not so much. There have been times when people heard the truth and ran to Jesus, and other times when they ran the other way. I have been wise sometimes and insufferable sometimes. In other words, I have been there, done that, and know that it is hard.

Hill Street Blues was a popular series in the Eighties about police in a large unnamed city and the Hill Street precinct in that city. Each morning, the officers would gather for the morning briefing by Sergeant Phil Esterhaus. After each briefing the last thing the sergeant always said was, "Hey, let's be careful out there!"

Let me say the same thing to you. In fact, it is good advice. Jesus said, "Behold, I am sending you out as sheep in the midst of wolves, so be wise as serpents and innocent as doves" (Matthew 10:16). In other words, you be careful out there.

Compromised Truth

Never compromise the truth. Paul's question to the Galatians is the experience of anyone who speaks truth: "Have I then become your enemy by telling you the truth?" (Galatians 4:16). Well, yes—and that should be expected. The sometimes-irritating nature of truth should never be the reason one does not speak truth. Only silly people expect that speaking truth in a reasonable and kind way will solicit praise. Frankly, the truth revealed to Christians—about traditional and important sexual standards, the family, social justice, racial matters, sin, right and wrong, etc.—is not always pleasant truth. Everybody gets angry at the weatherperson who forecasts rain.

When the late William F. Buckley started the conservative magazine *National Review*, he said that a conservative stands athwart history yelling "Stop!" at a time when no one is inclined to do so. Christians do that too. Our history of revealed truth is thousands of years old, has been tested and tried, and has been demonstrated to be a better way. It must be spoken and never compromised.

Needless Fights

"If possible, so far as it depends on you, live peaceably with all" (Romans 12:18) is also good advice. Have you ever met someone who seemed to always be looking for an argument? No matter what you say, you know that it is not going to go well.

I was once speaking at a Bible conference in Chattanooga. After one of the sessions, as I was standing in front of the church, I noticed a man in line who looked quite angry. Evidently, I said something that irritated him. The closer he got to me, the angrier he seemed. As soon as we were face-to-face, he started yelling. My friend Lea Clower (a big guy who was a former fighter pilot and drunk, and after his conversion, a preacher) came to my rescue. He went up to the man, put an arm around his shoulders, and said, "I think we need to have a little talk." The man did not want to talk. He wanted to yell—at me. Lea then helped him by taking him by the arm and walking him out a side door. I do not know what happened after that.

The man was a Christian but a very angry one. Unbelievers hardly ever listen to angry Christians. Or, if they do, it's only to respond in kind.

Shouting Is Only for Football Games

Shouting is a reflection of one's passion in sports, but elsewhere it is a reflection of one's insecurity. The only people who shout their truth are those who are unsure of that truth. Christians do way too much shouting. The writer of Proverbs said, "A soft answer turns away wrath, but a harsh word stirs up anger" (Proverbs 15:1). Someone supposedly said to Barry Goldwater when he was running for president that, of course, he needed to walk through the field, but he did not need to wave a red flag at the bull each time he did.

I have a rather deep voice, so sometimes I sound angry when I am not. One time I called home to speak to my wife Anna, and she was not there. I got the answering machine. I do not remember the message I left, but I closed with "Love you!" That day I got home before Anna did and listened to all the phone messages. As I listened, I was shocked by how angry I sounded. When Anna got home I asked her if I sounded that way all the time. "Well, yeah," she said laughing, "but it's okay. I know you, and know how you talk and love you." Just so you know, I have repented of my tone, and have tried to talk more gently with varying degrees of success.

The problem with unbelievers is that they do not know us, do not particularly love us, and are not willing to cut such slack for us. Christians must be so very careful. As suggested in the last chapter, we do not have anything to prove, protect, or push.

I have a friend with whom I often disagree. The other day he said to me, "If I disagree with you, can we still be friends?" What a great question and attitude. It is the attitude with which we should take our truth into the world. We should speak softly and let God carry the big stick if he wants. The big-stick stuff is way above our pay grade.

Some Things Are Indefensible

Paul said to his young friend Timothy that he should teach the doctrine he was given and not devote himself, or let others devote themselves, to "myths and endless genealogies, which promote speculations rather than the stewardship from God that is by faith" (1 Timothy 1:4). Paul was saying that Timothy should keep the main thing the main thing.

The Christian faith is complicated, but too often believers get caught up in the complications instead of the only truths that are important for those who do not buy it. Christians should always be saying—with their words and actions—that if anybody wants to be forgiven, loved, and accepted, they can be. I have a friend who says that awakening would come to the world when unbelievers no longer identified the Christian faith with guilt, moralism, and manipulation, but rather with forgiveness.

Everything that is a part of our Christian walk is a mixed bag. It is one of the implications of the fall. That mixed bag includes the church and its history (it is not always pretty), our faithfulness (we sometimes run), our obedience (sometimes we are not), public figures who do bad things and call themselves Christians (sometimes we do bad things and call ourselves Christians), and the public and formal stands of the church (often ill-advised). It is what it is. Properly understood, the Bible is clear about all of that. When our only goal is to defend the church, our own commitment, or that of our brothers and sisters, we fight a losing battle. That's why we should never do it.

Lights under a Basket

Sometimes Christians do too much hiding and ducking. Paul said that Christians should stand out in a dark world "as lights" (Philippians 2:15). Jesus then describes how Christians should light the world, "Nor do people light a lamp and put it under a basket, but on a stand . . . In the same way, let your light shine before others" (Matthew 5:15–16). I have a friend who told his seatmate on a plane about Jesus. That man said it was the third time that week on a plane that someone had told him about Jesus. "What's with you guys?" he said, "Does someone pay you to ride airplanes and talk about Jesus?" Nobody paid us, but we are everywhere. Too often I am just content to serve Jesus as a part of his secret service.

Jesus's command to let our light shine does not mean Christians have to wear a Christian T-shirt or put Christian books on their shelves. It also does not mean that we should wear our faith on our sleeve. It does mean that we have to show up and be who we are.

Someone has said that most of the world is run by people who simply show up. There is some truth to that. At minimum, Christians are people who need to show up. I am not talking about disasters, places of need, or mission fields. We already do that, because Christians are fairly good at compassion. I am talking instead about normal places that Christians too often try to avoid like neighborhood street parties, bars, local service clubs—or, even more important, at political discussions, organizations that lobby for social justice or racial equality, the local town council, or the refugee center.

The problem with secular culture is not so much the bad things that are promulgated, but that Christians have either hidden or fled to more comfortable places. That is true of almost all of pop culture. Christians have run and then thrown rocks back at those places.

What can believers do instead? Just show up. Christians smell like Jesus; they cannot help it. When Paul in Galatians 2:20 said that he was crucified with Christ and Christ lived in him, he was not giving Christians something to do or a goal toward which to work. Paul was expressing a fact, one that is true of every Christian. It does not have to do with how religious or good believers are; they smell like Jesus.

It is sort of like the compass good parents give their children—the compass that always points in the right direction. Children cannot get rid of it—and most try. Jesus is sort of like that in the life of every believer. If being a Christian means that Jesus is present where Christians are, then all they have to do is show up and, when the opportunity arises, not duck. That is all. It is the most effective evangelism program on the face of the earth—the mere presence of Christians.

I have some close friends who would be embarrassed if they knew I was talking about them. Paul and Cindy Rosarius run a tech company, Palm Tree Tech Center. The interesting thing about Paul and Cindy is that they have their fingers in almost every pie in the community. I met them when they were sponsoring a food-for-the-poor event, and later spoke at the banquet for a computer foundation where they provide refurbished computers for those who cannot afford them. But that is not all. There is not an event that takes place in our community (religious or secular) in which they are not involved and, more often than not, leading.

There is a magazine that promotes our community and the surrounding communities, and in the last issue, there were so many pictures of Paul and Cindy that they were on almost every other page. "What's with you guys?" I joked with them, "Omnipresent?" They did not even know what I was talking about and had no idea of the photos in the magazine. Paul and Cindy simply show up. Not everybody agrees with their Christian faith—they do not talk about it much but never hide it. I do not know anybody who does not respect them.

The Menace of Manipulation

In 2 Corinthians 4:2 Paul says that he and his colleagues had "renounced disgraceful, underhanded ways. We refuse to practice cunning or to tamper with God's word." Do you know why? They did not have to, because by "the open statement of the truth we would commend ourselves to everyone's conscience in the sight of God."

I understand Christians who promote meetings, create films, have evangelistic dinner parties, sponsor events, or take phony surveys that have the hidden agenda of Jesus. In fact, I have done a good deal of it myself. But Christians should avoid hidden agendas—even for the best of reasons. They have a tendency to cause nonbelievers to lose any trust they might have had regarding Christians.

Anti-Semitism is an important topic for me. In fact, a while ago, I spent a good deal of time in Israel doing research for a book on the topic. I never published my book, but during that time of research, I talked to a good many Israeli leaders, Holocaust survivors, and regular Israelis. I was trying to understand why Jews are so hated. One of the things I discovered was that a whole lot of anti-Semitism has its root in Christian theology and actions. The cry has been that "Jews killed Christ" and, because they did, any persecution of Jews is tragically justified.

Because I was so convicted of the horror of anti-Semitism, some friends and I began having dinner parties for Jewish friends and acquaintances. A part of the party was so we could ask for forgiveness for what had been done to Jews by Christians. Every Jew knows. They do not talk about it much, but they know. One evening at one of those dinner parties after I had asked forgiveness for what Christians had done, a prominent Jewish real-estate investor stood up and spoke. He started crying as he told of how, as a boy other kids would wait for him on his way home from school and would chase him with iron pipes yelling "Christ killer!" Then he turned to me and said, "I want to thank you. Whenever Christians speak of these things, there is always a kicker . . . and I waited for one from you. It never came."

Christians have too many "kickers." For instance, they establish friendships for no other reason than to "lead others to Christ." And when others find out, no wonder they are angry.

When Jesus said in Matthew 5:37 that our simple "yes" should be "yes" and our "no," "no," because anything else came from the evil one, he was speaking about this very point (among other things). Just speak truth. Do not spin it. Do not manipulate.

Listening to Be Heard

I once wrote a book called *How to Talk So People Will Listen*. Someone suggested that I do another one titled *How to Listen So People Will Talk*. I think someone already wrote a book with that title, but nonetheless, Christians need to listen. They need to understand.

When I was a pastor, the church leadership and I decided that one of the problems with our very bad relationship with the gay and lesbian community was that we never listened to them. We designated an evening at the church and invited a group of gay and lesbian acquaintances to come and talk with us. They were quite hesitant because most of them had had less-than-positive experiences with the church. But after a bit of persuasion, they came. The place was packed. We put chairs on the platform and my associate Kent Keller said to the congregation, "We are here to listen, so pay attention." Then he turned to the folks on the platform and said, "First, tell us your experience with the church in general and Christians in particular."

You should have been there. We did not compromise truth, but we did not speak it either. We just listened and asked forgiveness for Christians' hateful words and unloving attitudes. We also promised to do better, and we did better. It was surprising how many gays and lesbians started coming to the church, and how willing they were to hear the truth that their new friends spoke about Jesus.

How do you like rap music? What do you think of heavy metal music? What about contemporary art and dance? What about people with political differences? What about transgender people or marginalized folks? What about the homeless? What about the angry? How about cult members? How about abortionists and the pro-choice protesters? And pornographers and sellers of pornography? The list is almost endless. I am not suggesting that believers compromise biblical doctrines or standards, just that they affirm everybody who has been created in the image of God. And that *would* be everybody.

Assumptions and the Christian Witness

Never assume. One time, Jesus healed a man who was born blind and his disciples asked, "Rabbi, who sinned, this man or his parents, that he was born blind?" The disciples assumed someone must have done something really bad. Jesus told his disciples that their assumptions were spurious, and that the blindness had happened so that "the works of God might be displayed" (John 9:2–3). On several occasions, Jesus confronted his followers on the danger of making assumptions. He still does.

I believe that whatever you think God is doing in your life right now, he probably is not. His ways are so circuitous and his love so deep that believers sometimes forget that he is far more interested in them than in what they are doing. That is a good practice for Christians: we believers should be more interested in loving people than in what they are doing.

Just as we believers assume to know what God is doing in each other's lives, we assume we know what God (or the devil) is doing in unbelievers' lives. R. C. Sproul once wrote a book *The Psychology of Atheism,*[1] in which he suggested that belief in God was normal and that unbelief was abnormal. He was sort of reversing Freud's silly view of believers. Sproul said that if you look at unbelief in people, you will find something in the past of the unbeliever that was a traumatic event causing the unbelief. Sproul was right. The difficult thing is to know what that traumatic event was. So, believers should not assume.

But there are a number of other places where believers assume. For instance, Christians often assume that someone will never become a Christian; that all unbelievers are sour and unloving people; that unbelief is the result of thoughtful investigation; that unbelievers are bad parents, bosses, or friends; and that the world is made up of "us" and "them," and so we should never consort with the enemy.

Over the years I have watched young people from orthodox churches go off to become students at secular universities. In many cases, those students have been prepared to confront the secular, angry, evil, humanistic unbelievers who will be their professors. Numerous books have been written to warn and prepare Christian students for the war they will fight. I have noticed that many of those students end up leaving the faith of their fathers. It does not happen because the arguments of unbelievers are so cogent (they are not) or because the world, the flesh, and the devil are too strong for their young souls. Instead, one of the major reasons why they leave the faith is that their preparation told them that the bad people in the secular academic institutions were out to get them and destroy their faith. Some are. Most are not. When those students found out that they actually liked unbelieving professors who were often caring, compassionate, and kind, it became a major disconnect from what they had been taught. These students figured that if their preparers were wrong in this assumption, they were probably wrong about other important things too. False assumptions can destroy faith and silence a witness.

People really are people, whether they are Christian people or not. Everybody has a story, every angry person has a reason for his or her anger, and everybody is needy—including you. Of course, in our ranks and the ranks of unbelievers, there are people who are angry, demeaning, and obnoxious. Casey Stengel once said that the secret of success in managing a baseball team was to keep the five guys who hated you away from the four guys who had not made up their minds. Our task, as believers, is similar. It is a mix. When you as a believer talk to people, try to remember that almost all of them are dealing with the hard side of life, have questions, and have a need to be loved, forgiven, accepted, and respected.

I am not much of a people person. An elder in a church I once served told me that I was the only preacher he knew who did not want to know his neighbors and just wanted to be left alone. He suggested that I, at least, learn my neighbors' names. I took his advice and was quite surprised. I discovered that many of my neighbors were curious about my faith and wanted to talk about it. I found out that some of them were really hungry for truth and were not offended by it. I discovered that many of them were just waiting for someone to say something. From experience, let me suggest that you get to know your neighbors.

You might be surprised, too.

CHAPTER 13

The Rest of the Story

[S]traighten up and raise your heads, because your redemption is drawing near. (Luke 21:28)

When I first wrote this final chapter, it was titled "How to Lose Friends and Irritate People." My publisher, God bless them, suggested that the title was a rather negative way to end a book. They obviously had a point, so I have rewritten this entire chapter. Now the world will never read the profound insights and wise observations I made in the chapter that never got published. (I think I just heard the angels laughing. The fact is that the publisher did you a favor, and you did not even know it until now.)

In the original chapter, I wanted to make sure that this book did not become a pipe dream written by Steve the Pollyanna. I still do. While what I have written is true and practical (insofar as I am able), we believers really do not have to be as irritating as we often are. We do not have to defend secondary truth. We are often wrong in our political, theological, and social views. We should be sensitive to the culture in which we have been placed. And we should model the important truths of forgiveness and love everywhere. In other words, there are biblical attitudes and beliefs that should keep us from being insufferable—sometimes.

But not always.

I have a friend who says that anybody who makes his or her living with religion will lose either their religion or their livelihood. While that is quite cynical, there is some truth to it. Let me tell you something that is almost always true: Christians who care too much about what others think of their faith are in danger of losing both the faith and the friends. If you want to lose friends and irritate people, just believe, say, and live the truth of the Christian faith.

I have a close friend who, when he became a Christian, worried about his friends and how they would react to his new-found faith. I told him that that was the least of his worries. I said, "God will take care of that for you. You'll find that you have some real friends who will think you're crazy but will still be your friend . . . and the others will leave you alone."

Christians should never be surprised to discover that some people do not like them for no other reason than their Christian commitment. Frankly, if I were not a Christian, I would not like Christians much either. If Christian truth is true (and it is), it is not good news to people who want to be their own god or worship one more to their liking, who see themselves as the center of the universe, who believe that morality is determined by vote, and who see heaven as something that everybody deserves (with the exception of Hitler).

The theological giant Karl Barth wrote more than nine thousand pages of dogmatics (theology). His commentary on the book of Romans, in particular, was an explosion, devastating a lot of theological nonsense. Barth has been incredibly influential in both Roman Catholic and Protestant theological circles, and his influence on the entire direction of theological thought in the Christian world is beyond estimation. On a more personal note, when I was a student in a theological seminary where the popular theology was so far left that it almost did not matter, Karl Barth pointed me to Christ and, at the same time, gave me intellectual ground on which to stand.

There is so much more I would like to say about Barth, but I bring him up to make a point—well, two points. First, at the heart of Karl Barth's theology is the revelation of an unknown and unknowable God to humankind. Barth and another great theologian and his friend, Emil Brunner, broke fellowship over this very point. Brunner's suggestion that God could be discerned by reason and observation was greeted by Barth's famous essay, "*Nein!*" In other words, there is no way that human beings can know God except insofar as that God chooses to reveal himself to them.

Second, Barth's life was geared to what God had revealed. Once he saw truth, he could not unsee it. One of the chapters in my friend Mark Galli's wonderful book *Karl Barth: An Introductory Biography for Evangelicals* is titled "The Fighter." Barth was that. Mark quotes from Barth's diary, "Today I did a good deal of bashing up and got bashed up by plenty of people myself."[1]

Galli writes about Barth's decision, at the age of fifteen, to become a theologian,

> He didn't realize at the time the unhappy direction theology had taken in the nineteenth century, nor the desperate need to engage it with all the firepower a theologian could muster. Barth's martial character did not serve him well as a boy, but it became indispensable for the battle he would fight as a mature theologian. He would grow from a terrible child into an *enfant* terrible—a man whose unconventional theology (for the times) would embarrass his liberal mentors and change the course of church history.[2]

We believers are in the same boat. God has revealed to us his love, grace, mercy, and sovereignty. We did not get to vote on the truth he revealed. Then, God commissioned us to go out into the world and stand for, speak, and live out that truth in our lives. We should remember that our message will not make some people happy. There is always a battle in which we are called to be engaged. The issue is not whether we will lose friends and irritate people. The issue is, which friends and which people?

While I was working on this book, I attended the funeral service of a fine young Christian man, Jakin Foster. In the card that was given out at the service, there was a quote from Jakin: "When I die I want Satan to rejoice and be thankful that I'm no longer in the fight." I suspect that Satan did rejoice at Jakin's going home.

But there is more than the truth. The problem is that there is the love, too. We Christians have been loved without reservation or exception, and now we have found that we can love without reservation or exception. Truth and love are a pretty scary combination for Christians who want to be safe and never to offend. Of course, you can believe the truth and forget about the love part. But as C. S. Lewis put it:

> To love at all is to be vulnerable. Love anything and your heart will be wrong and possibly broken. If you want to make sure of keeping it intact you must give it to no one, not even an animal. Wrap it carefully round with hobbies and little luxuries; avoid all entanglements. Lock it up safe in the casket or coffin of your selfishness. But in that casket, safe, dark, motionless, airless, it will change. It will not be broken; it will become unbreakable, impenetrable, irredeemable. To love is to be vulnerable. The alternative to tragedy, or at least to the risk of tragedy, is damnation. The only

place outside of heaven where you can be perfectly safe from all dangers and perturbations of love is hell.[3]

Not a very pleasant alternative, is it? Damned if you do and damned if you do not.

Let me suggest that believers do what they have been called to do: go out into all the world. The world is sometimes antagonistic and angry, but God calls believers to love people, love God, and speak truth. That sounds so simple and easy, but it is not. Just the opposite—it is really hard. Jesus said, "Woe to you, when all people speak well of you, for so their fathers did to the false prophets" (Luke 6:26).

I thought that needed to be said. So now I have said it, and I feel better. It is a part of the rest of the story.

There is more to that story.

Luther said that Christians need to preach the gospel to each other, lest they become discouraged. He was right. In fact, Christians need to be reminded more than they need to be taught. When Peter says that Christians are a "chosen race, a royal priesthood, a holy nation, a people for his own possession," he is defining believers. Knowing who they are, Peter then says what Christians are called to do: "that you may proclaim the excellencies of him who called you out of darkness into his marvelous light" (1 Peter 2:9). Peter is saying to his readers, "Don't forget!"

The world says, "Have a drink, and forget." Jesus says, "Drink and remember." In fact, much of the Christian faith is remembering.

Remember Who He Is

When Jesus taught his disciples how to pray, he said that they should begin with these words: "Our Father in heaven" (Matthew 6:9). There are a lot of ways Jesus could have taught his followers to begin their prayers, but he chose this particular set of introductory words because he did not want them to forget the real God. Jesus was saying, "Don't forget that he's God—the sovereign Creator, Ruler, and Sustainer of all that is. Also, don't forget that he's your Father."

I wish you could have met my father. He was not a Christian until the last three months of his life, but even as an unbeliever people liked him a lot. You would have, too. He was kind, quiet, gentle, and loving, and had less self-righteousness than anybody I ever knew. He was also a bad sinner who knew it. In fact, the reason he did not become a Christian until very late in his life was because he did not think he was good enough. People lied to him about that, and he believed their lies.

Before my father became a Christian, I loved being around him. I remember the night I threw a cherry bomb at a house where an elderly lady was sitting on the front porch. I did not see her and—while it scared her spitless—she was okay. When my father found out, he loved me. He was not happy with me, but he went with me to the police, and then to the home where the lady lived so I could apologize. The whole time, he kept his arm over my shoulder and said, more than once, "I know it's hard, but *we'll* get through this okay." I remember Sunday mornings when my father—even having gone through a Saturday night bender—with one son under one arm and the other son under the other, would read the Sunday morning funnies to us. I remember how he kept a photo of his sons in his wallet and talked about his sons to anyone who would listen, showing them our picture. My late brother was a lawyer/district attorney, and I was a preacher. My father would laugh and say, "There isn't a problem I have that one of my sons can't fix." I remember sitting on the front porch with my father—he loved thunderstorms—and being held by him as the scary thunder rolled across the mountains. The thunder was not scary, because my father held me and loved the sound. To this day, I love thunderstorms, and I live in Florida where God shows off with lightning and thunder almost more than any other place in the world. Whenever there is a thunderstorm, I think of my father, and I think of God.

When Jesus said that believers should call God Father, I want to speak in tongues and dance. That is because I had an earthly father whose love was without exception or reservation. If you did not have a father like mine, let me give you permission to think of my father when you think of your heavenly Father. It could be that you had a demanding, angry, and abusive father who was never pleased with you. Maybe you assumed that God was like your father. He is not. He is like my father, and you can think of mine instead of yours when you remember who he is.

Remember Who You Are

There is an old sermon illustration about a king who had a hellion for a son. A long list of kingdom tutors had worked with the prince and the prince only got worse. Finally, a young man told the king that he thought he could help and was hired. After a week, there was an amazing and wonderful change in the prince. When the king asked the tutor what he had done that brought such a positive change in his son, the tutor said, "I pinned a piece of royal purple cloth on his shirt and told him, 'Remember who you are.'"

Preachers (me too, on occasion) have often used that illustration to urge people to obedience, faithfulness, and purity. While I suppose that may be appropriate, a better use would be for it to illustrate who Christians are—not what they should do. Too often faith is defined by doing. Even this book, I fear, could be that. If you continue to remind yourself about who you are—and allow God's Spirit and your Christian family to remind you—much of this book will be irrelevant. You are the son or daughter of the King. You are loved, accepted, and forgiven, without reservation or exception. Your Father, the King, will never let you go, never leave you alone in the dark, and never ask you to go anywhere or do anything where he will not stand with you. Actually, he always thinks that a party without you is not even a party. In fact, playing off the old Garth Brooks song, you can serve your friends in low places, because you have family and friends in very high places.

Do you remember where God found you?

I do. I remember the horrible guilt, loneliness, and fear. I remember what it felt like to be always on the outside looking in. I remember the shame. Then, I remember when he came. I remember the overwhelming love, forgiveness, and acceptance.

"You're free," he said kindly.

"What exactly does that mean? Can I say whatever I want to say?"

"Yes, you can say whatever you want to say. That's what it means to be free."

"Does that mean I can do whatever I want to do?"

"Yes, you can do whatever you want to do. That's what it means to be free."

"Can I go wherever I want to go?"

"Yes, you can go wherever you want to go. That's what it means to be free."

"Then," I remember saying to him, "I think I'll go with you."

I did. For all these years, I have been hanging out with him. I am still sometimes insufferable, self-righteous, and afraid. There are still so many things that need fixing. But I am better than I was because I remember who I am and where he found me.

Remember Who They Are

The most important thing to remember about Christian truth is that it really is good news to people who really do need to hear some good news. Andrew Petiprin, in his wonderful book *Truth Matters*, says that his book "champions truth, and asserts that the authentic teachings of the Christian faith are the best means of human flourishing. . . . In fact, it is my conviction that orthodox Christian belief is the only balm for our wounds in our inevitable times of distress . . . and it is also the joy of our hearts in times of blessing. It keeps us from thinking too highly of ourselves and also instills in us an infinite worth given by an all loving God."[4]

Later in the book, Andrew writes, "God wants you to be transformed, healed, and saved by his grace. His truth draws you to him like a magnet. It has been on offer forever, and it remains today the greatest bargain of all time. You do nothing but assent. You say 'Amen'—not just once, but throughout your life of faith. The true God who is never of your own making and who may frustrate you before he comforts you, will never leave you alone."[5]

I have mentioned this before, but non-Christians are not enemies. They are just like you.

There is a story about a gas station attendant who was approached by a newcomer to the town, and the guy asked the attendant what the people were like in the new town.

"What were they like in the place you lived before?" the attendant asked.

"They were jerks. I've never lived in a place I disliked more. Nobody cared, nobody spoke to anybody, and nobody went out of their way to help anybody. I'm glad I don't live there anymore."

"Well," the attendant said, "I'm sorry to tell you this, but you're not going to like living here much better than that place. People here are exactly the same."

Later on, another man, also a newcomer, came into the service station and asked the same attendant the same question. The attendant asked this man about what the people were like in the town where he had previously lived.

"Oh, they were wonderful," the newcomer said. "In fact, we hated to move. We made so many friends there. They were friendly and kind, and always willing to help. We loved living there."

"Then you're going to love living here, too. The people here are wonderful. You'll like them a lot . . . and they you."

There is a sense in which the Christian call makes speaking truth to the world an "us" and "them" project. But when we take that too far, it can truncate our witness. As is often said, if all you have is a hammer in your toolbox, everything starts looking like a nail. Once we believers demonize "them" and fail to remember their sleepless nights, the guilt that haunts them, and the pain they experience, the hammer becomes our weapon of choice.

Remember that they need what you needed. The only difference between you and them is Jesus. We had very little to do with that. We still do not.

Remember Who Empowers You

I have mentioned very little in this book about the supernatural. I repent of that, but I am not going back to rewrite this book. I will say it to you now: remember that the Christian faith is a supernatural faith. People in their right minds would never believe and live as Christians except for some kind of supernatural invention. Paul called following Christ foolishness (1 Corinthians 1:18), and he was right. But Christians do believe in Jesus, and the fact that we do is a fairly good indication that something is going on that is beyond us.

If aliens from Mars should land on earth and watch a television news program with all of the war, deprivation, poverty, death, destruction, hatred, division, and chaos reported therein, and then heard the Christian witness about a loving God, they would be convinced that we were fruitcakes. The fact that we really do believe in a loving God is not something that we would make up after observing the world. At best, we might believe in a creator God who has gone away on vacation—or at worst, a monster of a God. But a loving and benevolent God? No way. But Christians do believe, and that fact is an indication that there really is a loving and benevolent God.

Just as supernatural intervention is demonstrable in our Christian beliefs, it is also a supernatural act when we speak truth, it is heard, and someone runs to Jesus. A number of years ago, I had a friend who was not a Christian. I really liked her because, well, just because I did. I was not her friend to lead her to Christ, but with that being said, I wanted her to know Jesus, another friend of mine. I cannot tell you the number of times I managed to tell my friend the good news about Christ, and each time she looked at me as if I had lost my mind. Finally, I decided that I was going to try once more; after that, no more. So when the conversation warranted it, I told my friend about Jesus and his love for her. "Steve," she said to my surprise, "why didn't you tell me this before? That's so good." She became a Christian.

What happened? It was God's timing, God's action, and God's prompting. When it was time, it was time. To be honest, I felt useless—because I was. Well, maybe not exactly useless—I did, after all, speak the truth. But once I had done that, the ball was in my friend's court and God's court. That took a great load off my back.

You will find that there are divine appointments happening all the time. All you have to do is to speak truth, and do it in a kind and loving way.

A part of what I do is in media. Key Life is heard on hundreds of radio stations all over the country. We do a talk show, "Steve Brown, Etc." And we are online. I have a great voice (God's joke was to put this deep voice in this body). As a result of what I do, a whole lot of people think I am wonderful or, alternatively, think I am obnoxious. What people do not know is the great number of gifted and wonderful people who make possible what I do as the front man. They plan programs, handle the technology, write scripts, answer letters, answer questions, schedule, research, edit, handle criticism, and a thousand other things. The great thing is that I get the credit (or the blame) for what they do.

It is helpful to remember that when you speak truth, you do not stand alone either. All kinds of supernatural forces stand with you. No matter how poorly you speak that truth, no matter how horribly you live it, and no matter how little you know it, when you stand, angels stand with you, Jesus prays for you, and God directs it all.

In 2 Kings 6, the armies of Syria surrounded Elisha, who was staying in the town of Dothan. The king of Syria wanted to rid himself of this troublesome prophet. Elisha's servant, convinced that they were going to die, moved into a panic mode, "Then Elisha prayed and said, 'O LORD, please open his eyes that he may see.' So the LORD opened the eyes of the young man, and he saw, and behold, the mountain was full of horses and chariots of fire all around Elisha" (2 Kings 6:17). When you speak truth, the mountains, as it were, are still full of horses and chariots of fire.

That is a good thing to remember.

Remember the End of the Story

I have said a number of times in this book—with some significant caveats—that we Christians are right, and they are wrong. That is true, but we should keep in mind that there is more: we win, and they lose. While that is not something over which to rejoice, it is a good thing to keep in mind.

I have a friend who pastors in a city with a university. On the side, my friend serves as the chaplain of the university's football team. His daughter is a cheerleader for a rival university's football team. On one occasion, my friend's team decimated the team for which his daughter was cheering. On his side of the field, there was delirious celebration over the win. The players poured a barrel of Gatorade over the coach's head, the band was playing, and everybody was hugging and shouting. My friend was joining in. Then he looked across the field and saw his daughter standing on the sidelines crying. My friend said that it was very hard to celebrate when someone he loved so much was crying.

It *is* hard. We Christians should have some difficulty in celebrating our win. In fact, when truth is rejected and people prefer dark to light, every Christian should feel the profound pathos.

Still in the end, we do win. The win is so assured that the Bible sometimes speaks of it as if it had already happened. When Paul talks about the action of God in the life of the believer, he speaks in the past tense ending with "and those whom he justified he also glorified" (Romans 8:30). In Ephesians 2:6, Paul does the same thing, saying that God "raised us up with" Christ, and "seated us with him in the heavenly places." The Bible speaks of Satan as a previously defeated foe (Colossians 2:15).

Heaven is real. It is a place where we will not be insufferable, nobody will make fun of us, nobody will reject the truth we believe and speak, nobody will walk away, and nobody will debate us. The arguments will be over, the derision will be stilled, and the rejection will no longer exist. We will have all of eternity to share war stories, and we will have the mother of all parties.

Until then, let's tell the truth to as many people who will listen. We really want a big crowd at the party.

Endnotes

Introduction
1. Kendra Fletcher, *Lost and Found: Losing Religion, Finding Grace* (Greensboro, NC: New Growth Press/Key Life Books, 2017), 13.

Chapter 1
1. Wendell Berry, *Jayber Crow* (Berkeley, CA: Counterpoint LLC, 2001), 164-165.

Chapter 2
1. Sophia Lee, "Digital Sages," *World Magazine*, August 18, 2018, https://world.wng.org/2018/07/digital_sages.
2. Rick Warren, *The Purpose Driven Life* (Grand Rapids, MI: Zondervan, 2002), 17.

Chapter 3
1. Jake Luhrs, *Mountains* (Austin, TX: HeartSupport, Inc., 2018), 6.

Chapter 4
1. Reggie Kidd, *With One Voice: Discovering Christ's Song in Our Worship* (Grand Rapids, MI: Baker Books, 2006), 130.
2. Sarah Condon, *Churchy: The Real Life Adventures of a Wife, Mom and Priest* (Charlottesville, WV: Mockingbird 2016), 19–20.

Chapter 5
1. John R. Stott, *Christ the Controversialist* (Downers Grove, IL: Inter-Varsity Press, 1976).

Chapter 6
1. Calvin Miller, *An Owner's Manuel for the Unfinished Soul* (Wheaton, IL: Harold Shaw Publishers, 1997), 122. Emphasis added.
2. Martin Luther, *Saemmtlice Schriften*, Letter no. 99, August 1521, Vol. 15, cols. 2585–2500. Translated by Erika Bullmann Flores (St. Louis: Concordia Publishing House, n.d).
3. Martin Luther, "Heidelberg Disputation: Thesis 7," 1518.

4. John Calvin, "Calvin's Full Quote of God's Baby Talk," God Is Open, https://godisopen.com/2015/11/21/calvins-full-quote-of-gods-baby-talk.

Chapter 7

1. Jared C. Wilson, *The Imperfect Disciple: Grace for People Who Can't Get Their Act Together* (Grand Rapids, MI: Baker Books, 2017), 21–22.
2. Os Guinness, *Doubt: Faith in Two Minds* (Downers Grove, IL: IVP Books, 1976), 31.

Chapter 8

1. Brennan Manning, *The Relentless Tenderness of Jesus* (Grand Rapids, MI: Baker Publishing Group, 2004), 112.

Chapter 10

1. Tertullian, *The Apology,* Chapter XXXVII, Tertullian's Plea for Allegiance, A2, https://carm.org/tertullian-apology-part2.
2. Thomas A. Kelly, *A Testament of Devotion* (New York: Harper and Row, 1941), 108–9.
3. Kenneth Blanchard and Spencer Johnson, *The One Minute Manager* (New York: William Morrow and Company, 1980).
4. Ken Blanchard, "Catch People Doing Something Right," *How We Lead*, December 24, 2014, https://howwelead.org/2014/12/24/catch-people-doing-something-right.

Chapter 11

1. Bob Briner, *Roaring Lambs: A Gentle Plan to Radically Change Your World* (Grand Rapids, MI: Zondervan, 1994).
2. Jonathan Merritt, *Learning to Speak God from Scratch: Why Sacred Words Are Vanishing—and How We Can Revive Them* (New York: Convergent Books, 2018), 6.

Chapter 12

1. R. C. Sproul, *The Psychology of Atheism* (Minneapolis: Bethany Fellowship, 1974); republished as *If There's a God, Why Are There Atheists?* (Ross-shire, UK: Christian Focus Publications, 2018).

Chapter 13

1. Mark Galli, *Karl Barth: An Introductory Biography for Evangelicals* (Grand Rapids, MI: William Eerdmans Publishing Company, 2017), 13.
2. Ibid., 18.
3. C. S. Lewis, *The Four Loves* (New York: Houghton Mifflin Harcourt, 1971), 23.
4. Andrew Petiprin, *Truth Matters: Knowing God and Yourself* (Greensboro, NC: New Growth Press, 2018), 7.
5. Ibid., 149.